THE WORLD'S FASTEST MOTORCYCLES

THE WORLD'S
FASTEST
MOTORCYCLES

MICHAEL SCOTT & JOHN CUTTS

CHARTWELL
BOOKS, INC.

A QUINTET BOOK

Published by Chartwell Books Inc.,
A Division of Book Sales Inc.,
110 Enterprise Avenue,
Secaucus, New Jersey 07094

ISBN 1-55521-001-5

This book was designed and produced by
Quintet Publishing Limited
6 Blundell Street, London N7

Art Director Peter Bridgewater
Editor Louisa Young

Typeset in Great Britain by Central Southern
Typesetters, Eastbourne
Manufactured in Hong Kong by Regent
Publishing Services Limited
Printed by Leefung-Asco Printers Limited
Hong Kong

The authors and publishers wish to thank the following for
permission to reproduce illustrations:

All-Sport Photographic Ltd 8, 26-7, 42-3 i; BMW (GB) Ltd 44-7, 106-7;
Malcolm Bryan 48-9 i, 124-5; Alan Cathcart 123; Kel Edge 11 b, 28-9,
33-7, 48-9 c, 50-51 i, 56-7c, 61 a, 64-5, 90-91, 92-3 c, 96-101, 116-7,
119-120; Honda (UK) Ltd 21 b, 62-3 r, 64-5 br, 68-9 b, 111 r; *The
Illustrated Encyclopedia of Motorcycles* edited by Erwin Tragatsch
6-7, 40-41; Kawasaki Motors (UK) Ltd 10, 11 a, 21 al ar, 70-71, 109 l,
110, 111 l, 113 c b; Mitsui-Yamaha 22-23 al, 80-81 c, 84-5 c, 86-7 r, 88-9,
109 r, 112; Andrew Morland 24 c, 38 i, 118; Don Morley 16, 17 al, 18-19,
26-7, 58-9, 68-9 a, 92-93 r, 113 a; Michael Scott 114-5, 122-3; *SuperBike*
14-5, 16-7 b, 20, 22-3 ar, 24 a ar, 25 b, 31, 38 c, 40-41 a, 42-3, 50-51 c,
53-5, 56-7 r, 60 c, 61 b, 62-3 c, 66-7, 74-5, 76-7 a, 78-9, 80-81 i, 82-3,
84-5 i, 86-7 l, 102-3, 104-5 c r, 108; Suzuki Motor Co. Ltd 2-3, 12-13,
22-3 c, 76-7 b, 104-5 l.

i = inset; a = above; b = below; c = centre; r = right; l = left.

PAGE 2-3: Suzuki's RG500 — grand prix bike on the road.

CONTENTS

For Learner and Expert

PREVIOUS PAGE: *Velocette — a tradition of big booming singles.*
RIGHT: *To many, Honda's CBX Six remains the definitive superbike — six cylinders, twin camshafts, 24 valves, and a glorious disregard for common sense.*

HIS *is* the golden age of motorcycling. The contemporary motorcycles profiled in this book are the fastest, most powerful two-wheelers of all time – ultimate dream machines with such sparkling specifications and dizzy performance levels that their very existence would have been unimaginable a few years ago. If the 1970s was the era of the original superbikes, the 1980s will be remembered for the arrival of genuine racing replicas – 160mph racing bikes made into street hardware – motorcycles so awesomely powerful, plain quick and specialist that they are simply authentic racers with headlights. Racing has not only improved the breed but created a new genus of bikes – grand prix replica speedballs for the street.

What are they like to ride, these fabulous, fire-breathing roadburners? Despite a top speed capability that is virtually unusable outside a proper race-track, these exotic machines are safer and easier to ride than ever before. There have been huge improvements not only in engine development and power output but also in the cycle components – the wheels, tyres, frames, suspension and brakes. The bikes are getting lighter yet stronger, more manageable and robust. They handle confidently, steer responsively, brake better and hold the road with impressive authority. Riding a modern sports bike is like flying. Rider and machine are as one, the rider becoming an extension of the motorcycle, hands operating the throttle, steering and brakes, feet selecting gear ratios, the whole body controlling stability and direction, head tucked in down the straights, knee out and dragging in the corners, transferring body weight for the perfect line through every bend. The lure and thrills of the open road on a fast bike are more attractive, exhilarating and intoxicating than ever, offers an irresistible mixture of speed and power, force and momentum, danger tempered with skill and grace. The throttle still goes both ways but it opens wider and gets on the gas harder and quicker these days.

Development has been astonishing. Big bike enthusiasts around the world are bedazzled by the glittering choice of sports weapons now available. The four-stroke market is currently dominated by 150mph 750s, such as the Suzuki GSX-R and Yamaha's FZ, liquid-cooled inline fours making 100bhp and lots of redline rpm. Their power-to-weight ratios are also quite exceptional. For the lightweight Suzuki, the 100bhp package weighs just 388lb. Suzuki's 130bhp/434lb GSX-R1100 is even more remarkable. These are power-to-weight ratios simply unobtainable in the car world, except at the very highest level of competition. At the top end of the four-stroke market, the litre and litre-plus bikes, the state of the art is 160mph performance. The trend is

undeniably towards the lighter 750s and middleweights but the inevitably large and bulky 1100s still rule the outright top speed stakes.

In the two-stroke world, the blue riband road racing class, the 500cc Grand Prix, have bred a copy-cat war of 500cc stroker GP replicas. The Yamaha RD500, Suzuki RG500 and Honda NS400 are wonderfully faithful renditions of successful factory racers – V4s, square fours and V3s, making lots of rev-crazy, peaky-as-hell power, fearsome acceleration and short-fuse liveliness. Fortunately, they are all equipped with frames and suspension tough enough to contain the excessive horsepower.

The cross-over between race bikes and road machines is now complete. People have always raced road bikes in production classes but now any aspiring private racer can easily and quickly transform an out-of-the-crate road machine into a competitive World Championship Endurance or Formula One mount. Whatever part you look at on a modern bike, the influence of the race-track is obvious. From the aerodynamic lines of the screen to the construction of the few inches of rubber that are the bike's only contact with the road, racing parallels are manifest, enhancing the overall performance. The wheels are smaller and lighter for less unsprung weight and quicker steering. The tyres have become fatter, low-profile, wide-section, more adept at holding the road and coping with the wheel-spinning acceleration. Radials are finally making an appearance on top dog sports bikes. The brakes now feature dual-piston calipers biting on floating discs while the front forks are equipped with anti-dive systems as well as separate pre-load and rebound damping adjustment. The forks are large-diameter, often with a brace between the legs to resist flex. Rear suspension is monoshock, which weighs less and rules out the imbalance inevitable with two shock absorbers. The single dampers are fed by a variety of rocking arms and linkages – Uni-Trak, Full-Floater, Pro-Link and Monocross. Some are rising-rate, all are extremely efficient at dealing with the bumps. Ride quality and suspension are probably *the* most significantly improved features of the last five years of mass-production motorcycles.

Frames, still traditionally the preserve of small specialist builders, are also receiving more attention and design consideration. Double steel cradles are still commonplace but increasingly the trend is towards using the engine as a stressed frame member. Aluminium beam-type frames, as developed and campaigned in Grand Prix races, have naturally found their way onto the street-legal replicas. Aerodynamic studies have paid dividends in making a motorcycle more slippery and streamlined at speed as it cuts through the air, often against the wind. Fairings, screens, fork legs, mudguards and bodywork are now integrated to achieve the lowest possible drag coefficient. For a big bike an efficient fairing may be worth something like the equivalent of 25bhp and 20mph at top speed.

There is also pure speed engineering – engine development and the relentless pursuit of horsepower. All modern two-strokes are fitted with exhaust power valves to help spread the power, giving both a high rpm top end *and* a usable mid-range. Combustion chambers have all been redesigned for maximum volumetric efficiency. On four-strokes, less than four valves per cylinder is unusual (Yamaha's FZ750 has five) and more valve area means the gas can be worked on faster. Valve trains are still typically chain-driven DOHC but gear-driven cams can be found on Honda's VF750 and 1000R. Carburettors come in all shapes and sizes, feeding V4s from inside the vee and inline fours from above the motor by downdraft induction. Usually they are of compact, constant vacuum design; others have flat sides. All are ultra-responsive under every operating condition. Ignition systems have been completely transistorized for some time – the very best work with computer-controlled digital fuel injection. Exhausts vary from the almost ubiquitous four-into-two with balance pipe, sometimes with complex cross-over headers, to the maximum grunt of four-into-one exhaust plumbing with a large collector. Clutches are increasingly becoming hydraulically operated; Honda's version even has a one-way release mechanism to avoid rear wheel lock up during quick downchanges. Cranks, cams, con rods and pistons are being made lighter yet stronger. The use of exotic, lightweight materials from magnesium or carbon fibre is becoming more affordable and thus more commonplace.

As for horsepower itself, nobody really knows where the ceiling lies. At least one manufacturer, Kawasaki, have declared that they will never build a faster bike than their GPz1000R, a fabulous 125bhp inline four with a top speed genuinely in excess of 160mph. Around the world, safety-conscious watchdogs, legislators and governments have viewed the escalating horsepower wars with alarm. In Europe many countries have adopted a 100bhp limit. In pursuit of power and speed, the major manufacturers may have already paved the way towards the extinction of these ultimate sports machines. Does anybody really need a 160mph road bike?

Meanwhile, motorcycling goes on at the speed of life itself. The bikes in this book were not built as utilitarian commuters or run-arounds, they were constructed around one guiding principle and are united by one

single, serious purpose – maximum mph motorcycling. In every red-blooded enthusiast's dream garage, there are a number of motorcycles – one for the street, another for the long tour, a dirt bike perhaps, certainly a flash-looking café racer plus a couple of out-and-out sport tools. The machines on the following pages are strictly the best – the world's fastest and the world's finest. Nothing on the road can live with these bikes. They are in a different league – higher, untouchable, unique and immaculate, but accessible and available. Pull on a helmet, zip up those colour co-ordinated leathers, take a deep breath, turn the key and go for it. Motorcycling may never be this good again.

SUPERBIKING MILESTONES

HE word superbike came out of the 1960s. In one sense it was a cliché, a buzz-word, but in another it was a specific term for an actual concept. A superbike is a machine conceived not for sound reasons of common sense, but in a hedonistic celebration that combines the exhilaration of fine engineering with the wild joy of unfettered speed; a celebration of an excess of horsepower over horse-sense. A superbike is a vehicle that nobody needs but that every red-blooded motorcyclist wants.

The concept is older than the word. It has been an intrinsic part of motorcycling since the first sporting gent, his flat cap worn rakishly peak to the rear, endeavoured to have a single cylinder that chuffed more powerfully than his neighbour's. Once, the legend goes, there were only two motorcycles in the world. The faster was the original superbike.

They were not just reckless toys, those distant Indians and Harleys, those Broughs and Vincents, the Moto Guzzis and the MV Agustas. They have served a broader interest than the thrills of the foolhardy few. As a forcing house for ideas and a field for engineering endeavour they have inevitably borne a fruit of excellence. Once, a twin overhead camshaft design of four cylinders was the epitome of rarity and extravagance of design. Today, the same engine design is commonplace on public roads.

There have been glamorous aberrations along the route: V-twins in great profusion, asymmetrical three cylinder designs, two-strokes and four-strokes. Even today, the inline four is not quite the definitive design . . . V3s and V4s, square fours, and the long-lived V-twin all appear among the fastest bikes.

By tracing the landmarks of design (including the significant deviations) the evolution of the modern superbike becomes clearer. A historical perspective may also make the directions taken by the next generation a bit less surprising.

The modern superbike began with the Brough Superior of the 1930s. It was a machine much like the others of its day, but with something extra. In the fashion of the times, the engine was a proprietary unit, usually a JAP V-twin. George Brough, who had a keen eye for what would make his machines stand out, made the rest. He included some fine detail engineering, plenty of spit and polish, and engine tuning to ensure a good turn of speed. There was nothing *mechanically* outstanding about the machines – their honour came from their performance, and a perceived superiority to their rivals.

It was later that metallurgy and better design were combined, and British manufacturers began to compete with each other in the specifications of their own

engines. The pre-war motorcyclist had such variety to choose from as the Matchless Silver Hawk (a narrow-angle V4, all cylinders contained within a single block), Brough Superior's flat-four Golden Dream, the Square Four Ariel, the straight-four American Ace, and the purring two-strokes of Alfred Scott in Yorkshire.

One of the great truths of motorcycling is that design is self-regulating. Because motorcycles lean over to go round corners, there is a strict limit on almost every aspect of design. Every motorcycle, from humble commuter to out-and-out racing machine, uses the same technology.

The superbike's nearest relative is often the grand prix race bike. Thus it was, when motorcycle racing came to be dominated (for more than two decades spanning the war years) by Norton's 500cc single-cylinder racer, known as the Manx Norton, that the definitive road superbikes also had one cylinder. Naturally enough, the most desirable of them all was a Norton, which shared the racer's engine – detuned to make it more manageable for the road. This was the 500cc Norton International, a long-lived sports road bike with a single overhead camshaft, genuine 100mph-plus top speed, and a fine pedigree.

The Inter sired many imitations, and not all of them had the Norton's credentials. Two in particular achieved a legendary status in spite of having their overhead valves operated by pushrods: the BSA DBD34 Gold Star, and the Velocette Venom. Like the Norton, these were 100mph machines, with deep bellowing exhaust notes and accurate steering and roadholding. Cynics say that these qualities were the result more of very limited suspension movement and not much weight than any particular inspiration of design.

These were not particularly easy motorcycles to live with. Starting the engine, for instance, was a business that demanded a stout heart and an even stouter leg on the kickstart. It is no easy task turning over a big, high-compression piston fast enough to ensure that it will fire up and keep running, and start-up was a carefully orchestrated and timed ritual that included full use of the valve lifter/decompressor lever and manual retardation of the ignition. Even so, many were the ankles strained and calf muscles gouged by a backfiring big single.

In the 1950s the single-cylinder was deposed from automatic racing victory by the Italians, with their four-cylinder machines from Gilera and MV Agusta (not to mention the illustrious though not particularly successful V8 from Moto Guzzi, the most complicated and evocative racer of all time). By now the roadgoing superbike had grown in size from the premier racing size of 500cc, and had diverged.

Ton-up heroes of their lifetimes: blue-chip investments today.
ABOVE: *1951 500cc Norton International — a racer with a headlight.*
ABOVE RIGHT: *Fishtail silencer and sculpted engine casings on the classic 500cc Velocette Venom of the 1960s.*
OPPOSITE ABOVE LEFT: *Primary colours and four-leading shoe drum brakes for the 1973 MV Agusta.*
OPPOSITE ABOVE RIGHT: *Triumph Bonneville — the legend lives on.*
BELOW RIGHT: *The immortal, beautifully functional 1951 1,000cc Vincent Black Shadow.*

Again, it was the British manufacturers who led the way. The Triumph Speed Twin (actually a pre-war model) set the pattern for a generation of superbikes: parallel twins with overhead valves (but not overhead camshafts) which rapidly settled on 650cc as the optimum size, and which continued to rule the roost for almost two decades.

The course of development of the Speed Twin is typical. Designed by the legendary Edward Turner, it was introduced as a 500cc model in 1938, and grew to 650cc in 1950. In 1959, the immortal twin-carburettor Bonneville was born (the name was acquired after a Triumph broke the world land speed record at the Bonneville Salt Flats in the USA). The Bonnie was probably the best-known motorcycle of its generation. Ultimately it grew to 750cc, surviving in the process the collapse not only of the original Triumph firm, but also that of the workers' co-operative that succeeded it. Perhaps its finest incarnation was that produced by the co-op, the 750 Eight-Valve. Despite its qualities the machine was overcome by circumstances and came to nothing.

The generation of parallel twins had many revered denizens. One was the Norton, which like the Triumph saw its final flowering as a promoted 650 – the Dominator grew into the 850 Commando. This had electric start and a novel way of controlling what was the parallel twin's greatest bugbear, engine vibration. Norton's Isolastic system let the engine shake about, but isolated the rider by rubber-mounting not only the power unit, but also the rest of the power train including the rear pivoted fork.

Into the Seventies.
ABOVE RIGHT: *Triumph's three-cylinder 750cc Trident was fast but temperamental. The final version has disc brakes and an electric starter.*
OPPOSITE ABOVE RIGHT: *Norton added the same items to their venerable parallel twin, disguised the vibration, and called it the Commando. Both bikes were the last of their line.*
BELOW RIGHT: *The bike that caused the panic was Honda's CB450 nicknamed the Black Bomber. With twin camshafts, soaring revs, and new levels of performance, it changed the way the world looked at motorbikes.*

Among the BSAs, the Royal Enfields, the Matchlesses, AJSs, Triumphs and Nortons of the post-war generation, there was one British motorcycle that rose above them all. Exclusive and expensive, it was the definitive superbike of its time. The Vincent (the tank badge carried both words) was certainly faster than anything else around and incorporated many design features that were years ahead of its time. One such was the rear suspension, which used a triangulated structure operating springs and dampers located under the seat – a system that predated Yamaha's monoshock by two decades. But it was the engine that made a legend of The Vincent. It was an all-aluminium overhead-valve V-twin of 1000cc with a broad spread of power, and it could lope along relaxedly at 100mph, and gallop to 125mph or more. The Vincent was rather too expensive for its own good, however, and the firm ceased production at the end of the 1950s.

In the USA, the superbike ethic had gone its own way. By this stage there were only two manufacturers of note left: Indian and Harley Davidson, and the former was soon to perish. This left Harley, who sustained their reputation for robustness without breaking any performance records, and continued to build large-capacity low-revving V-twins as if nothing was happening anywhere else.

Through the 1960s, American riders bent on high performance had to rely on imported British bikes, or perhaps (if they were rich and lucky) an MV Agusta, a complex twin-camshaft four-cylinder piece of exotica based closely on the same firm's racing models. Meanwhile Japanese manufacturers were gathering strength, and Honda, Suzuki, Yamaha and the late Bridgestone were showing that 350cc bikes need not necessarily be much slower than 650s.

At the end of the decade the British industry had one last kick at building a superbike – a three-cylinder machine with a 750cc engine and an exhaust note that sent a shiver down your spine. It came in two forms, the Triumph Trident and the BSA Rocket 3. The latter had the engine canted forward, and its racing versions were invincible. However, its specification was old-fashioned, with push-rods operating the overhead valves, and furthermore it was complex to manufacture. In the face of the rising tide of Japanese superbikes, the Trident/Rocket was unable to hold its own, and, having survived from 1969 until 1977, was one of the final casualties of the dying but still complacent British industry.

The Japanese had begun by manufacturing machines in the smaller capacity classes, but in the mid-1960s they served notice that they would not limit themselves for ever. The machine that was the herald of things to

come was Honda's CB450, dubbed the Black Bomber, which startled the motorcycling world with more than just its sophisticated engine. It challenged the established order of 650 twins by offering greater performance from a smaller engine. This was achieved because of the engine's capacity to rev way beyond the accepted ceiling of around 6,500rpm, and to top out at a giddy 9,500rpm. The engine design was a race-bred twin, and included twin overhead camshafts and ingenious torsion-bar valve springs.

Honda had more to come. In 1969 they introduced the machine that changed the world – the CB750. Four cylinders, four carburettors, four exhaust pipes, and a disc brake – it was a revelation both in terms of design and performance.

Until then, the only modern four-cylinder motorcycle had been the MV Agusta. The Honda was quite different. It was a motorcycle for everyone, the father of the modern superbike, and it marked the start of the new golden age. At 100mph, with almost 15mph still to go, anyone riding a Honda could afford to laugh at someone trying to keep up on an out-of-breath British 650. Only the Triumph Trident could hope to match it, on a good day. But there were three other Japanese manufacturers with an interest too, and they were not going to take this lying down.

Suzuki gave the first reply, with a machine that was quirky then, and remains quirky in retrospect. Their empire was founded on buzzing little two-strokes, the largest being a nominal 350cc (actually 315cc). Suzuki's first superbike was also a two-stroke, of a new breed.

The Golden Age begins...
ABOVE: *Honda's CB750 of 1969 was the first four-cylinder superbike from Japan.*
ABOVE RIGHT: *This close-up shows the widely copied design.*
OPPOSITE ABOVE LEFT: *Contemporary Kawasaki MachIII three cylinder two-stroke was different — light and lethal.*
OPPOSITE ABOVE RIGHT: *The seminal 900cc Z1 followed on, and was rather more than a Honda copy with an extra camshaft. Its big four-cylinder engine was the toughest and fastest anyone had ever seen, and stayed in production for more than a decade.*
BELOW RIGHT: *Ten years later, Honda's CB1100R was little different in basic design, but a long way on in performance, with more than 140mph, racing streamlining, and superb roadholding and braking.*

Three water-cooled cylinders across the frame earned the bike the soubriquet Kettle and purple-and-white paint proclaimed it as something special. Performance was similar to that of the Honda, and the GT750 was developed into a successful racing machine, campaigned (among others) by Barry Sheene.

Kawasaki were by now a rising force and set out to outperform these new monsters of the road. They also chose three-cylinder two-strokes, but stayed with air-cooling to keep weight down. Their 500cc MachIII became a legend: erratic roadholding and acceleration so vivid that the blue smoke it left behind might as well have come from the tyres as the three exhausts. This was only the start.

Kawasaki's MachIV was a 750cc machine based on the same design principles, but even faster. This machine introduced the average road rider to the wheelie: it was almost impossible to *stop* the front wheel lifting off the road as the two-stroke power came on with a snap through the gears.

Honda had not merely led the way, they had started the fashion. Their four-cylinder across-the-frame four-stroke became the standard of the Japanese industry through the 1970s. First to follow were Kawasaki, with the double overhead camshaft Z900 of 1971, which gave rise to a generation of bikes that peaked in air-cooled form with the sporting Z1R (or perhaps the later GPz1100, the first motorcycle with fuel injection) and continues to the present day with the liquid-cooled GPz range. Next to follow were Suzuki, whose GS750 and then GS1000 were very similar to the Kawasakis in basic design. However, they started a trend towards integrated styling with their 1100cc Katana of 1981,

which has an angular fairing that blends into the fuel tank.

Honda, in the meantime, continued to refine their designs, adding twin overhead camshafts and race-developed chassis components. Probably the finest of their air-cooled fours was the CB1100R, a limited-production 1981 model that was designed with production bike racing in mind. Its standards of braking, road-holding and performance showed how much could be achieved with more care, money, and the use of more exotic materials than were practicable in mass production.

Most exciting of the breed of big Japanese fours were their sporting variants.
RIGHT: *Yamaha's XS1100S — a shaft-drive heavyweight with some of the flab removed.*
OPPOSITE LEFT: *Kawasaki's Z1R immortal in more ways than its apparent indestructibility.*
BELOW RIGHT: *Suzuki's GSX1100 Katana, first of the high-fashion sports road-bikes.*

Yamaha were the last to join the trend for four-cylinder monsters and they jumped in in a big way. Their XS1100 was the biggest bike yet, when it arrived in 1974, and was subtly different as well as extremely heavy. It used shaft drive instead of the ubiquitous chain, and car-style vacuum control for the ignition advance to give a widespread of lazy but plentiful power. More a tourer than a sports bike, the XS1100 was still a gigantic performer, with a top speed approaching 130mph.

While the British industry simply collapsed under this onslaught, European and American manufacturers regrouped and fought back. In the case of Europe, the tactic was predominantly to continue to do what they were good at – building machines of robust simplicity compared with the Japanese complexity, achieving comparable performance through light weight and refined roadholding.

Italian Batallion — and a grand Dutch oddity.
ABOVE: *The Laverda Montjuic was a thinly disguised racer — throaty exhaust, harsh suspension, a high-revving six-speed 500cc twin engine, and an urge for the fast life.*
ABOVE RIGHT: *Holland's Van Veen OCR was pricy, potent, and very heavy. Premature termination of its Wankel Rotary engine, borrowed from a proposed Citroen car, also killed the bike.*
RIGHT: *The Ducati 900SS could also switch from road to track with few changes — here the long-legged and stable vee-twin tackles the Isle of Man.*
OPPOSITE RIGHT ABOVE AND BELOW: *Italy also produced the first ever six cylinder superbike. It was a 750cc Benelli, here in a later, more stylish 900cc guise.*

The shining example came from Ducati, who designed a smooth and beautiful V-twin with exotic desmodromic valve gear (dispensing with springs to close the valves mechanically). It was at first a 750, but grew to 860cc (nominally 900), and later to a full 1000cc. Its finest expression was in the 900SS, a spartan and slender sporting bike of the mid-1970s that introduced many riders to the integrity of race-style roadholding (and the discomfort of race-style suspension).

Still in Italy, Moto Guzzi perfected a range based around a 750cc (later 1000cc) V-twin engine that was disposed with the crankshaft lengthways, using shaft drive. The pushrod engine had been designed as a military pump unit, but made a fine motorcycle unit in spite of its pedestrian origins – pumping out massive torque at relatively low rpm. The machines live on.

Moto Guzzi had been historic stalwarts of motorcycling; Laverda were newcomers, the progeny of an agricultural equipment firm. They also stuck to two cylinders at first, relying on exacting engineering to make the most of their overhead-camshaft designs. Their first superbike was the 1969 750S, but it was the production-racing SFC that made their name – stripped for action, painted a vivid orange, and with a deep-throated bellow from the twin exhausts. The 500cc twin-cam Montjuic of the late 1970s was the natural child of the 750SFC. Laverda's bid for superbike glory was reinforced in the mid-1970s by their big three-cylinder twin-cam range. This was produced in sizes as large as 1200cc, but it is the 1000cc Jota that became a legend, a brutish machine which was raucous, firmly sprung, and very, very fast. MV Agusta, meanwhile, continued to refine their four-cylinder twin-camshaft model, cul-

minating in the glorious 850cc Boxer, beautifully styled and as exotic as ever.

Europe's largest manufacturer was BMW, who throughout the 1970s remained true to their original concept of 1928: a simple pushrod flat twin, crankshaft disposed longitudinally for shaft drive, with the well-cooled cylinders poking into the wind. Refined over the years, this model reached its ultimate in the R100RS of 1975, a 125mph-plus machine of rare quality and beauty. Relatively light, mechanically simple and quiet, the 1000cc RS boasted as its chief distinction a fairing designed in a wind-tunnel to give the best combination of streamlining, aerodynamic stability, weather protection and looks yet achieved. Although it has been replaced by the three- and four-cylinder BMWs, the R100RS remains a machine of classic elegance.

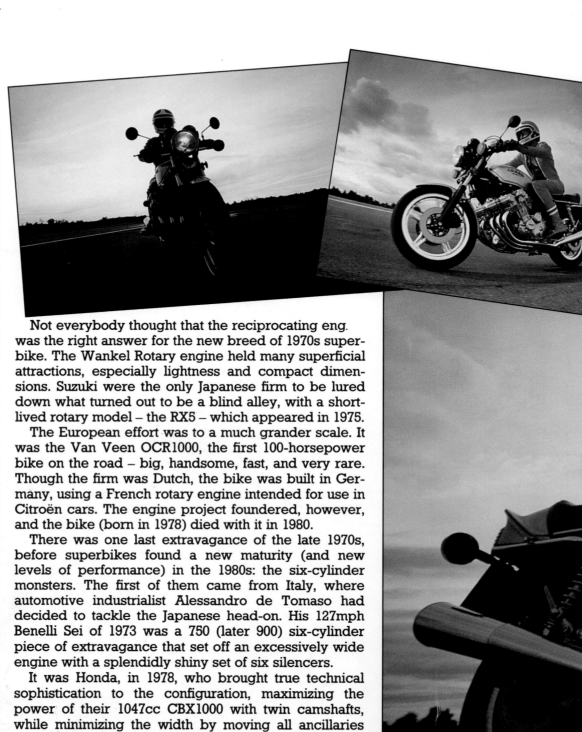

LEFT, RIGHT AND BELOW RIGHT:
Three views of Honda's remarkable CBX1000 — six cylinders, 24 valves, with a top speed of almost 140mph. Nothing like it had been seen before, nor had anything been heard like the muted screech at 9,000rpm. Honda's big six proved two things: first, that it could be done; and second, that it could be done better by a lighter four cylinder bike.

Not everybody thought that the reciprocating eng. was the right answer for the new breed of 1970s superbike. The Wankel Rotary engine held many superficial attractions, especially lightness and compact dimensions. Suzuki were the only Japanese firm to be lured down what turned out to be a blind alley, with a shortlived rotary model – the RX5 – which appeared in 1975.

The European effort was to a much grander scale. It was the Van Veen OCR1000, the first 100-horsepower bike on the road – big, handsome, fast, and very rare. Though the firm was Dutch, the bike was built in Germany, using a French rotary engine intended for use in Citroën cars. The engine project foundered, however, and the bike (born in 1978) died with it in 1980.

There was one last extravagance of the late 1970s, before superbikes found a new maturity (and new levels of performance) in the 1980s: the six-cylinder monsters. The first of them came from Italy, where automotive industrialist Alessandro de Tomaso had decided to tackle the Japanese head-on. His 127mph Benelli Sei of 1973 was a 750 (later 900) six-cylinder piece of extravagance that set off an excessively wide engine with a splendidly shiny set of six silencers.

It was Honda, in 1978, who brought true technical sophistication to the configuration, maximizing the power of their 1047cc CBX1000 with twin camshafts, while minimizing the width by moving all ancillaries away from the crankshaft ends. The alternator, for example, was mounted behind the bank of cylinders. With 105 horsepower, almost 140mph on tap and a rev ceiling beyond 9,000rpm, the Honda Six had as much technology as anyone had ever seen on a motorcycle. It progressed from a supersports model to become a fully-faired gentleman's express, but was superceded by Honda's (and other people's) four-cylinder models. It was simply too complex for its own good.

In the 1980s only one six-cylinder model remains, Kawasaki's massive Z1300 (qv). Technical complication for its own sake is now a problem of the past, in this age of efficiency. Only the power has gone on increasing.

THE BIKES

bimota

PREVIOUS PAGE: *The Ducati Pantah 750. Italy's finest — exclusive Bimotas are handbuilt in small quantities for well-heeled connoisseurs. There are frames for a variety of four cylinder Japanese engines, but standards are too high for a 'one-size-fits-all' general purpose frame. Each engine gets its own specially tailored tubes.*
RIGHT: *The latest Suzuki SB4 poses alongside its SB3 predecessor.*
INSET: *The new bike goes into spectacular action.*

BIMOTA SB4

BIMOTA have the distinction of making the world's most expensive motorcycles. They are hand-made, bespoke creations using all the very best components. They are labour intensive to make, beautifully finished and very fast. Bimota make exclusive, expensive, luxurious sports bikes that approach motorcycle perfection, that ideal but elusive marriage between Japanese horsepower and a frame that can deliver the goods. Take one large Japanese powerplant and place it in a unique frame with the best suspension, wheels and brakes money can buy.

The SB4 is built around Suzuki's GSX1100 with the engine carried by Bimota's chrome-moly, semi-cradle that supports the motor from the sides with the top tubes unusually joining ahead of the forks and steering head for extra rigidity. The swing-arm and rising-rate, rear suspension are anchored to the frame by a huge plate of Avional 14, an aircraft quality alloy. This crucial structure is milled from a solid block, glued and then bolted in place, all in pursuit of the perfect steering head/swing-arm relation. The frame plus swing-arm weigh just 35lb.

It is light and low on the move with 16in wheels fitted with low-profile radial tyres. Bimota are the only company to fit radials as original equipment rubber. Suspension is by Ceriani telehydraulic forks with seven-way adjustable rebound damping and a De Carbon unit at the back. The rear rocker arm and all the linkages are lovingly made, rose joints and quality alloy details are everywhere.

The motor is stock except for a four-into-two Bimota exhaust and some extremely high gearing. The tall ratios complement Bimota's aerodynamic fairing and bodywork to achieve high speed and give the GSX1100 full top end expression, 150mph and *still* pulling.

The riding position is uncompromising and built for maximum speed work. The rider is stretched, fully prone, reaching down to the clip-ons across the broad back of the tank, feet high on the rearsets, knees tucked into the tank cutaways. It is cramped but strangely comfortable.

Everything about the Bimota sparkles with quality. Little is cast, it is all either machined from solid or press-forged with TIG welding throughout. The bodywork is all in fibreglass-reinforced plastic and fits like a glove. The bike exudes class and confidence.

The later SB5 uses the bigger 1135cc Suzuki engine but is essentially unchanged except for a longer wheelbase and different weight distribution. The one outstanding difference is the provision of a dual seat. Previous Bimota bikes had all been strictly solo machines.

BIMOTA SB4	
Engine	Suzuki GXS1100, air-cooled, DOHC, 16 valve, inline four
Cubic capacity	1075cc
Maximum power	112bhp at 8750rpm
Bore × stroke	72 × 66mm
Gearbox	five-speed, constant mesh
Final drive	roller chain
Dry weight	466lb
Top speed	155mph
Standing quarter mile	11.9sec
Date of launch	1983

bimota

RIGHT: *First all-Italian Bimota, the Ducati-powered single seater was an instant hit. Novel body styling enclosed the V-twin engine...only exhausts protrude, and is the same for road or racing versions. If any bike is destined to become a classic, the DB (Ducati Bimota) is it.*

BIMOTA DB1

WHILE their high standards of engineering and artistic design were beyond reproach, the Italian specialists at Bimota came in for some criticism at home for producing motorcycles with Japanese engines. The DB1 is their reply – an all-new, all-Italian masterpiece, with innovative all-enclosing bodywork that embraces the V-twin Ducati engine and Bimota's own frame in sensuous curves.

If the styling catches the eye, it is the exhaust note that tears at the heart-strings ... a mellow *basso profundo* that is part wistful and part defiant. To anyone over 30 (and a few others besides) the DB1 sounds like a *real* motorcycle.

Two versions of the DB1 were launched simultaneously in 1985. The first was pure racer; the second a road-going version with a headlight up front and a licence plate at the rear. It is also a little quieter and a little milder-mannered in the way it delivers the horsepower. The DB1 was an instant hit, and because of the production quantity envisaged, Bimota were able to offer it cheaper than their previous Japanese-based models.

The DB1's heart is the Ducati Pantah engine, a smooth 90-degree V-twin with exotic desmodromic valve gear, stretched to the full 750cc allowed by Formula One racing rules. Made in unit with the five-speed gearbox, the engine is suspended from a complex frame made of a trellis of short, straight tubes. In Bimota's fashion, the frame structure runs forward of the steering head, to brace it on all sides. The rear fork pivots from the gearbox casings, making the engine unit part of the frame. The front forks are Bimota's own, and the rear suspension has a rising-rate linkage to a single spring and damper unit.

On the move, the Bimota DB1 shows its pedigree at once, reflecting the care and experience in its design and construction. Pin-sharp steering and forgiving handling are the legacy both of the V-twin's low centre of gravity and of design expertise; these qualities in the DB1 must be felt to be believed.

The DB1 is fast, deceptively so, due to the relaxed way the twin-cylinder engine delivers its power. The speedometer reading is often a surprise on a DB1, as is the tireless way it sustains high average cruising speeds as well as fast circuit lap times.

Such an uncompromisingly sporting machine cannot be for everyone. Even in roadgoing form, the DB1 is strictly a single seater; and engine access is something of a chore, even though the body panels are quickly detachable. The ride is rather firm and there is certainly nowhere to strap any luggage.

BIMOTA DB1	
Engine	90 degree, V-twin. SOHC, desmodromic valves
Cubic capacity	748cc
Maximum power	70bhp at 8000rpm
Bore × stroke	88 × 61.5mm
Gearbox	five-speed
Final drive	chain
Wheelbase	53in
Dry weight	352lb
Top speed	133mph
Standing quarter mile	12.0sec
Date	1985

CAGIVA

RIGHT AND OPPOSITE ABOVE RIGHT:
Neat new bodywork and a big bore job for Ducati's 500cc Pantah engine gives the stylish Alazzurra performance and penetration to go with superb roadholding. Designed to broaden the rather specialist appeal of the Ducati, the Cagiva still retained exotic desmodromic valves.

CAGIVA 650 ALAZZURRA

WHEN Cagiva took over the ailing Ducati factory in 1983 they inherited some sporty models, among them a peach of a middleweight motorcycle, the Pantah V-twin, available in 500 and 600cc guises. After a long gestation period during which Cagiva (now the fifth largest bike manufacturer in the world) decided what to do with its prized Ducati engines and frames, there emerged a brand new motorcycle – the 650cc Alazzurra.

Adopting a dual range policy, Cagiva decided that the large capacity, sports Ducatis should still be developed as traditional, enthusiasts' machines and sold under the Ducati banner while Cagiva themselves would market the Pantah range as a fast but more civilized all-rounder.

The 650 Alazzurra (meaning 'blue wing' in Italian) is a bored and stroked version of the 600 Pantah, essentially unchanged but brought right up to date and fulfilling the company's ambition to appeal to more riders than the specialist, sporting Dukes. It is a lovely roadster. The toothed-belt driven SOHC and desmodromic valve operated engine is both lightweight and fast-revving for an Italian twin. The power it makes is smooth, torquey (it will pull from 1500rpm in any gear) and vibration free. Fed by incredibly large 36mm Dell Orto carburettors with accelerator pumps, the 650's broad powerband and responsive performance sets a benchmark for all other four-stroke twins. It is typically high-geared but nowhere near as tall as the 600 Pantah. Cagiva have certainly strengthened and improved Ducati's notoriously weak clutch.

No such improvement was needed with the frame, an inimitable steel trellis with the engine stressed and suspended beneath it. The frame consists of four cross-braced tubes arranged in two ladders, one each side running from the headstock down to the top of the crankcases. At the back the swing-arm pivots inside the gearbox casing as close to the drive sprocket as possible. The rear suspension is dated these days in using two shock absorbers but the handling is wonderful. This was always the Pantah's trump card; a classic combination of a revolutionary frame, a short wheelbase, low weight and quick steering. The Alazzurra dives into corners with impeccable manners, rock-like stability and oozes confidence. Roadholding and lean angles are exceptional. It has perfect poise and balance.

Where Cagiva could make significant improvements they have. Ducati were unbelievably lax about such things as control cables, instruments and electrics (including the ignition). Items like the seat and controls

CAGIVA 650 ALAZZURRA	
Engine	air-cooled, 90 degree, V-twin
Cubic capacity	649cc
Maximum power	56bhp at 7500rpm
Gearbox	five-speed, constant mesh
Final drive	roller chain
Wheelbase	58in
Dry weight	396lb
Top speed	130mph
Standing quarter mile	13.0sec
Date of launch	1984

were always spartan on a Duke, a bit of an afterthought, and Cagiva have sensibly introduced much more civilized and considerate rider amenities. Whether they have also softened Ducati's racy, ultra-sporting image is a different question. Certainly they have brought the legend up to date. The frame-mounted fairing and distinctive styling are all Cagiva's work, aiming to make the bike more popular and appealing in the world's markets. It has been a laudable exercise. What was always good about the Ducati Pantah is alive and kicking and its many, niggling faults have been largely eliminated. The Alazzurra is an attractive, alter-native middleweight for those looking for something different.

DUCATI

RIGHT AND INSET: *Last of the* **real** *motobikes? A soulful bass exhaust wakes the neighbours, but is music to the ears. Ducati's Mike Hailwood Replica echoes the great man's legendary TT victory in racing colours, as well a with its classic long-legged V-twin motor and desmodromic valves.*

DUCATI MHR MILLE

THE Ducati MHR Mille is a racing legend. In 1978 a many times World Champion named Mike Hailwood made a fairy-tale comeback aboard a beefed-up street bike and against all odds won one of the most prestigious races of all time – the gruelling, six lap, 226 mile Formula One TT on the Isle of Man.

Hailwood's bike was a hastily-cobbled together factory Ducati which beat much more powerful fully-fledged Japanese racers on its way to the chequered flag. Ducati were so pleased with the success, they released a limited edition of Mike Hailwood Replica (MHR) machines shortly afterwards. That bike was a 90 degree, V-twin of 864cc capacity, a design essentially unchanged since 1975. A lot of troubled water has flowed under Ducati's bridge since then. They were taken over by Cagiva and their 500, 600 and 900cc engines and frames have been updated and restyled, and are now sold under the Cagiva banner.

In 1984 however, a bike was launched to thrill every Ducati lover the world over – a 1000cc MHR, a bored and stroked version of the popular 900MHR, bigger and better than ever.

The big V-twin's calling card has always been massive torque. The bike has tall gears and long legs while the motor sports two of the biggest pistons in captivity. It is not a high-revving engine but makes plenty of power low down, in a relaxed, unhurried manner. The new 1000 machine has been substantially updated and comes with revised bevel drive, Nickasil barrels, a hydraulically operated dry clutch and a new, one piece, nitrided crankshaft running in plain bearings. In perfect primary balance, the 90 degree V-twin still features Ducati's original desmodromic valve operation with rockers that both open *and* close the valves.

The frame is a delicate-looking but immensely strong and rigid open spine type cradle using the crankcase as a structural member. The large full fairing hides the skeletal, rather elemental profile of the bike though nothing can disguise its thunderous performance.

There is nothing frantic about riding a Ducati even on an open road. The low frontal area and a very long wheelbase give excellent stability and roadholding.

The Ducati is a pure, unadulterated thoroughbred; a lean and hungry racer, one of the last *real* motorcycles. Many have described the essential Ducati experience as being akin to riding God's own motorcycle. Despite its considerable charisma and the myths and folklore that have sprung up around it, it is a fact that in the real world, a large Ducati is as fast on a tar road, point-to-point, as any comparable bike. Long may Ducati continue to flourish.

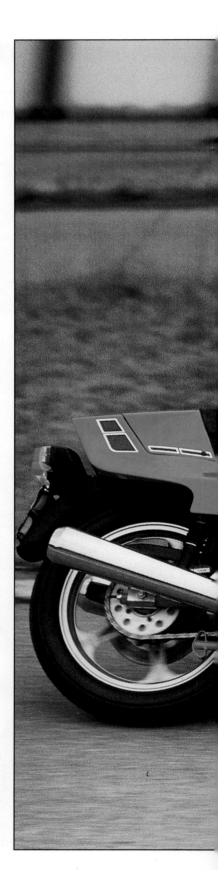

DUCATI MHR MILLE	
Engine	air-cooled, 90 degree, V-twin
Cubic capacity	973cc
Maximum power	76bhp at 6700rpm
Bore × stroke	88 × 80mm
Gearbox	five-speed, constant mesh
Final drive	roller chain
Wheelbase	59.5in
Dry weight	502lb
Top speed	137mph
Standing quarter mile	12.7sec
Date of launch	1984

DUCATI

ITALY

RIGHT: *Apart from the headlamps this is a close copy of the machine that won four world championships for Ducati. Race-standard equipment is expensive, but performs beautifully.*
INSET: *The floating-disc brake system, and damping adjustment on the front fork legs.*

DUCATI FORMULA ONE 750

THIS bike is strictly limited edition – a 750cc Formula One replica of the machine the factory raced in F-One and Endurance World Championships. It is essentially a big version of the bike which won four consecutive F-Two World titles for Ducati – a 600cc Pantah-engined and Verlicchi-framed V-twin. The racers were individually assembled at the small factory race shop, and in their spare time the race mechanics knocked up a few 750cc replicas for the road. Each is an expensive, hand-built, luxurious proposition for connoisseurs only.

The Pantah derived motor is well-oversquare and short-stroking, with two valves per cylinder, desmodromically operated by inverted tooth belts. Valve timing is lazy but Ducati have completely revised their combustion chamber shape for flame efficiency. It revs high and is long-legged; at just under 140mph the engine is turning 8900rpm. The claimed power output is only 65bhp compared to 80 or 90bhp for the real racers. After-market, go-faster options are easily available. The bike itself is not. The frame is minimalist, a space frame in round steel alloy tubing with the engine hanging below and stressed. Equipped with harsh, unforgiving, heavy-duty suspension, it is set up purely for high-speed stability and handling, where the ride is perfection. The steering is slow and offers little lock, so around town and at slower speeds even posing has its problems. The dry weight of the cycle is very competitive – 380lb contained in a compact 56.6in wheelbase. On an open road, the bike creates its own bend-swinging pace, running as if on rails in eager pursuit of the next thrilling apex. A Ducati on full noise and at maximum wick is a sweet and delectable riding experience.

This may well be the last pure Ducati. Since the takeover by Cagiva, the era of the big Duke sports bikes may be coming to an end. If so, then the F-One race replica is a fine, final example of the unique Ducati art – lightweight, V-twin motorcycles with beautifully smooth power and exemplary roadholding and handling. In addition it is the fastest production four-stroke V-twin in the world.

DUCATI FORMULA ONE 750	
Engine	air-cooled, OHV, 90 degree, V-twin
Cubic capacity	749cc
Maximum power	64.5bhp at 7900rpm
Bore × stroke	88 × 61.5mm
Gearbox	five-speed, constant mesh
Final drive	roller chain
Wheelbase	56.6in
Dry weight	380lb
Top speed	139mph
Standing quarter mile	12.6sec
Date of launch	1985

BELOW RIGHT: Italian style at its most svelte, with bodywork abbreviated to show the robust fins and casings of the air-cooled three cylinder engine. The original RGS introduced the line.
ABOVE RIGHT: The Corsa realised its full 140-plus potential.

LAVERDA RGS CORSA

THE Laverda lineage is that of a noble late arrival. The brothers Laverda built their first motorcycle, a 750 twin, in the 1960s. With success on the race-tracks, it won them a reputation for high performance and good engineering. Then came the 1000cc triple, typified by the raucous and very rapid Jota. With its 180-degree crankshaft – two pistons up, one down – the first generation triple was also somewhat raw-boned. Some vibration, as well as an enigmatic exhaust note, was the inevitable result.

Laverda eschewed such compromise engineering as balance shafts, and made sure everything was well made and well screwed together. When they tackled the vibration in order to tame the wild thing they had created, they did so with a major re-engineering job.

On the current 'second-generation' triples, not only is the engine mounted in rubber, the crankshaft is now 120 degrees (with all pistons evenly spaced). It has smoothed out more than the exhaust note.

The RGS is the result, and the Corsa is its sporting incarnation; a bike that clothes the punch of three big pistons in the sleekest of sheaths.

The bike is, as far as possible, a two-wheeled equivalent of a designer Italian sports car, with a twin-camshaft rev-hungry engine and RG-Studios original and aerodynamic bodywork in the classically elegant mode . . . a veritable Ferrari on two wheels. Tell that to a man who is experiencing the high-speed performance of the one-litre Laverda, and he will scoff at the insulated remoteness of a car-borne equivalent. One hundred and forty mph really feels like it when the wind is plucking at your back, and you can hear the distinctive wail of the robust three-cylinder exhaust note being swallowed up in your wake.

The process of civilization has given the RGS a quieter engine and a more subdued exhaust, to go with the new tailored image, not to mention new noise regulations of the 1980s. Not that that RGS is subdued. With 95 horsepower and a wind-cheating shape, it can run with the best of them, and top 140mph. The Jota's bad manners and vibration (as well as some of its urgency) have gone, replaced by a maturity that has broadened the power band to compensate. The later, smoother Laverda engine pulls strongly from low to high revs, and is well-mannered all the way.

Price as well as breeding separates the Laverda from the Japanese opposition. It is significantly more expensive, and in some ways rather old-fashioned. It has, for example, traditional twin rear shock absorbers, where its Oriental rivals have multi-adjustable rising-rate linkages operating single units.

The performance figures did not keep pace with the power war. The Italian factory at Breganze is too small to play that game. However, their market is among connoisseurs, who know that a bike with a good standing-quarter-mile time and a fearsome top speed is not necessarily better at traversing long distances at sustained high average speeds than a well-bred, well-balanced and amply powerful Italian thoroughbred.

LAVERDA RGS CORSA	
Engine	inline, three-cylinder, DOHC
Cubic capacity	981cc
Maximum power	approx. 95bhp at 6500rpm
Bore × stroke	75 × 74mm
Gearbox	five-speed
Final drive	chain
Wheelbase	60in
Dry weight	532lb
Top speed	142mph
quarter mile	12.3sec
	June 1983

MOTO GUZZI

ITALY

RIGHT: *A long-lived classic, Moto Guzzi's Le Mans takes an engine originally designed as a military pump into the realms of the 140mph superbikes. Robust simplicity, light weight, very tall gearing and plenty of mid-range power are the key-notes of a rapid but relaxed roadburner; exclusive linked brakes make it good at slowing down too. The latest version has crisp angular styling.*
INSET: *Earlier bikes reflected more curvaceous fashions of the time.*

MOTO GUZZI LE MANS 1000

THE Le Mans has been Moto Guzzi's top sports bike for over ten years. The big bore 1000cc version is a recent and welcome addition to the ranks but is essentially similar to the 850 Le Mans they have been producing, virtually unchanged, since 1977. The bike has a fine and enviable reputation as a tried, trusted and proven motorcycle. Its design may be dated and the main features are undeniably conservative and traditional. Reliability above all however has won it many friends and admirers.

The 948.8cc OHV V-twin engine with its longitudinally-mounted crank and shaft drive is not, by any stretch of the imagination a high-revving unit. Low down acceleration and pick up is dismal, unaided by unbelievably tall gearing and a dry, twin plate clutch. Once into its mid-range stride though, with the huge 40mm carburettors really roaring, it makes strong and plentiful power. Top end performance is the long-legged Le Mans hallmark and the high gearing helps it to a blistering top speed of over 140mph with the tachometer barely showing 8000rpm.

Stability and roadholding are very impressive, the bike is surefooted and responsive, a thoroughbred Italian stallion. The double cradle frame has the sump suspended between the down tubes with the engine weight carried low. Equipped with traditionally harsh, twin shock suspension, the only concession to modern chassis design has been the recent adoption of a 16in front wheel wearing a fatter tyre, making the Le Mans quicker-steering than ever. As befits one of the original café racers, everything about the bike is set purposefully low, making for a keen centre of gravity and a lovely, balanced feel.

Moto Guzzi's integrated braking system is still unique among modern motorcycles and is a boon to safety. The front and rear brakes are linked so that the foot-pedal operates both the rear brake and one of the front discs for measured, controlled braking. A special distribution valve directs 70 per cent of the pressure applied to the left hand front disc and the remaining 30 per cent to the rear. The front handlebar lever brakes the right hand front disc but need only be used from very high speeds.

Overall, the Le Mans is a traditional, curiously idiosyncratic bike with heavy yet strong controls, an agricultural yet unburstable engine and redoubtable Italian handling. The paintwork and finish are excellent. It is a sportsman's motorcycle, a high-profile and ever-popular machine that has long delighted enthusiasts around the world with its tireless performance and peerless reliability.

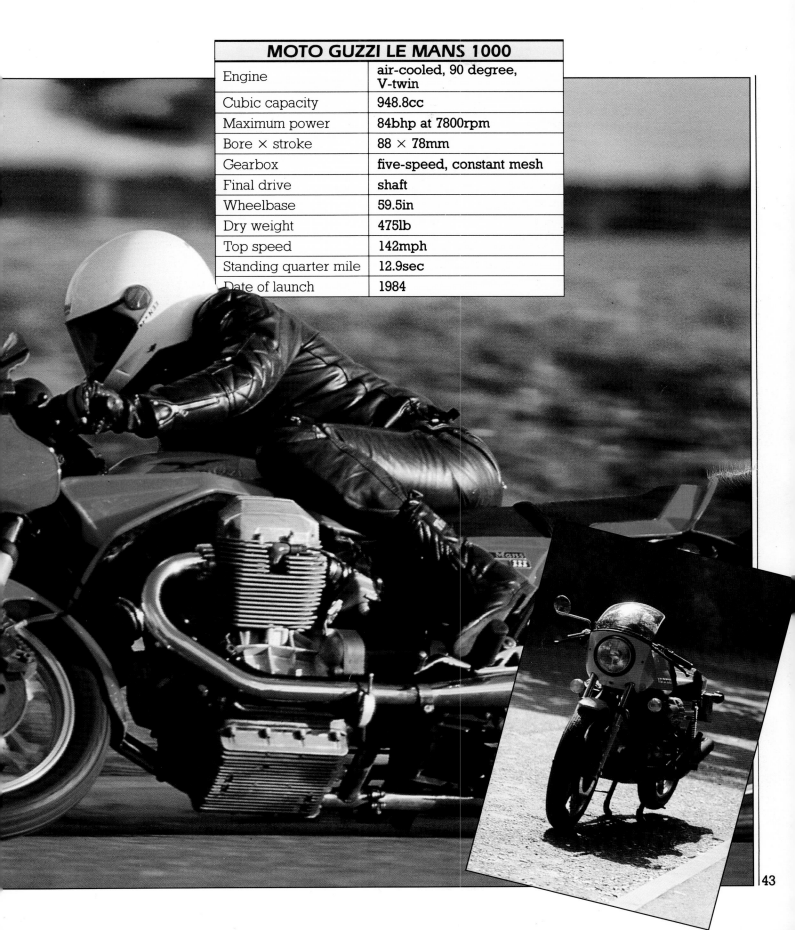

MOTO GUZZI LE MANS 1000	
Engine	air-cooled, 90 degree, V-twin
Cubic capacity	948.8cc
Maximum power	84bhp at 7800rpm
Bore × stroke	88 × 78mm
Gearbox	five-speed, constant mesh
Final drive	shaft
Wheelbase	59.5in
Dry weight	475lb
Top speed	142mph
Standing quarter mile	12.9sec
Date of launch	1984

RIGHT AND OPPOSITE: *Aristocrat, or should it be 'technocrat', of speed, BMW's styling is austere, but aerodynamically effective; horizontal cylinders keep the mass of the fuel-injected, electronically triggered engine slung low. Refinement means it can sustain high speeds in comfort for longer than many 'faster' bikes.*

BMW K100RS

HE K-series was the solution to a serious dilemma that faced Europe's largest motorcycle manufacturer in the early 1970s, and the K100RS is its leader. BMW had relied since 1928 on a single engine design – the horizontally opposed 'Boxer' twin. They had almost made an art form of this smooth, simple and well-cooled engine, fitted invariably with shaft drive.

In the meantime, however, the tastes of the motor-cycling public had been re-educated by the Japanese. An increasing majority preferred multi-cylinder designs, sacrificing light weight and simplicity for the extra power of three, four, or even six cylinders.

With falling sales BMW had to think again, and the answer was plain. They too had to build a multi-cylinder machine, or die. They needed to find a different approach if only for psychological reasons. The Bavarian firm could not be seen to be copying the Japanese. The new K-series models in 1983 showed that BMW had succeeded. Like most of its rivals, the new bike has a 1000cc inline four cylinder engine, with twin overhead camshafts. The similarity ended there.

In place of the normal mounting, with the engine cross-ways and the crankshaft at the bottom, BMW turned convention 90 degrees and laid it on its side. The engine bulk is now suspended beneath the frame, with the cylinder head on the left, and the crankshaft on the right.

To keep the overall height of their so-called 'compact drive system' to a minimum, the clutch is driven from a jack-shaft beneath the crankshaft, and the five-speed gearbox is mounted low at the back of the unit. Counter-rotation of the clutch is used to eliminate the torque reaction that rocked the bike to one side when the throttle was blipped.

This new design gave 90bhp, with a smoothness and quietness the old Boxer twin could not match. The K-series did retain two of the advantages of the flat-twin engine: a low centre of gravity, and shaft drive.

BMW borrowed from their car division for the latest in electronic engine management techniques. The K-series led the world with computer-controlled fuel injection integrated with the ignition, which gives ample smooth power and efficient fuel economy.

BMW built a fine rolling chassis for the compact 'Flying Brick' engine. In fact, the engine forms parts of the frame, with the single rear suspension arm pivoted on the castings. An inverted cradle of short straight tubes provides the superstructure which is clad in a choice of body styles reflecting rather quirky Teutonic styling, along with the fine finish and aerodynamic

design already associated with the BMW range.

It was not surprising that a world sated with an apparently endless stream of new models from Japan should have turned to the BMW with a sense of relief. At last there was a bike that could challenge the Japanese directly on performance that would not be rendered obsolete in the space of a few months. The K-series was an instant success, and its dynamic qualities deserved no less. Ultimate performance had perhaps been sacrificed for a well-rounded power delivery, but this is no drawback on the road. With its good weight distribution the bike also handles very well, and manages not to sacrifice comfort. There is a choice of models that covers the spectrum without over-proliferation: the plain, unadorned K100; the RT, with a big touring fairing; and the sporting RS, whose aerodynamic fairing seems to make it more stable as the speed climbs towards its maximum, close to 140mph.

BMW K100RS	
Engine	inline, horizontal, four-cylinder, DOHC
Cubic-capacity	987cc
Maximum power	90bhp at 8000rpm
Bore × stroke	67 × 70mm
Gearbox	five-speed
Final drive	cardan shaft, crown-wheel-and-pinion
Wheelbase	59.7in
Dry weight	492lb
Top speed	138mph
Standing quarter mile	12.4sec
Date of launch	December 1983

GERMANY

RIGHT: *A Range-Rover on two wheels — the BMW gives the smart set the facility for off-road riding, yet is a sensationally good street or city bike. At better than 100mph flat out, it is far faster than more specialized off-road bikes, though it pays a penalty in the weight of its 800cc engine. On a long dirt road with a reasonably good surface, there is nothing to touch the Bee-Emm — and its comfortable as well.*

BMW R80GS

THE R80GS earns its place in this collection by being one of the world's biggest and fastest off-road bikes. It is *very* good on the road but not so good on the dirt. The GS stands for *Gelanden Strasse* or street scrambler. BMW call it 'a hobby bike, a two-wheeled Range Rover' and the comparison is appropriate. It is not a serious dirt bike but it is one of the best all-purpose bikes ever built. Suitably beefed-up factory versions have won the gruelling Paris to Dakar rally on three occasions. In stock production form, the GS80 has proved a popular choice for riders exploring the world on long distance trips across continents with all types of terrain. It is a 100mph road bike that can cope with the rough stuff. The machine is an imaginative mix of parts that were already available on other BMW bikes, spiced with some adventurous engineering. An example is BMW's patented 'mono-lever' rear suspension, a one sided swing-arm with a single gas shock unit. In effect, it is half a swing-arm, but BMW's engineers made it both lighter *and* 50 per cent stronger than a conventional assembly. The rear wheel is held on by three bolts, there is nothing you could call an axle. The wheel bearing is big, the crown wheel housing is internally stressed since it has to carry the full loads of the back wheel with 6.7in of travel available, and the whole rear suspension works admirably. Quick wheel changing is obviously a bonus.

The front suspension consists of leading axle forks offering a luxurious 7.9in of travel. The bike is tall and needs to be for reasonable ground clearance (8.58in). The steering is quick and the throttle response lively. The whole machine is light and nimble with plenty of power and very good brakes. Like all flat twin BMWs, it has a low centre of gravity, so the bike can be chucked around with abandon. The dual-purpose, knobbly tyres are S-rated and give wonderful grip. The engine is an updated variant of the R80 road bike endowed with typical BMW performance – bags of torque and a wide spread of power – plus some dual-purpose innovations. The bike has a light-weight clutch and flywheel for quicker throttle response, and some low gearing; necessary for a dirt bike but lots of fun anywhere since it helps the GS to wheelie easily. On the open road it will hold 100mph for as long as the rider can face sitting up so high and exposed against the wind. Unfortunately what makes it good on the tarmac tells against it on the dirt. The bike is just *too* big and *too* powerful. Fully gassed (4.3gal) it weighs 410lb, fine for a road bike but a little heavy for serious off-road use. In addition there is the long wheelbase, the unsprung weight of the driveshaft and two horizontal cylinders that stick out a

BMW R80GS	
Engine	air-cooled, OHV, horizontally opposed twin
Cubic capacity	797.5cc
Maximum power	49.4bhp at 6500rpm
Bore × stroke	84.8 × 70.6mm
Gearbox	five-speed, constant mesh
Final drive	shaft and crown-wheel-and-pinion
Wheelbase	57.7in
Dry weight	368lb
Top speed	105mph
Standing quarter mile	13.8sec
Date of launch	1980

long way, all factors that conspire against its dirt ability. These are not problems when traction is positive on firm ground but in mud and real rough stuff, the bike bogs down far too easily.

The R80GS is best used as a cross-country bike, sticking mainly to proper roads but taking the odd short cut and back road where necessary. Above all else, the bike is a lot of fun to ride; it is a functional, practical, rugged and reliable all-rounder. Recently, various BMW importers have released Paris–Dakar replica versions of the bike as a tribute to one of the world's most successful desert racers.

GERMANY

RIGHT AND INSET: *The Krauser-BMW MKM1000 is one man's dream brought to reality. A frame built by the Messerschmidt aero-engineers gives unprecedented levels of sporting roadholding to the versatile BMW flat twin engine, while an eight-valve head releases extra power to match. A rare experience, on road or race-track. Note the one-piece bodywork.*

KRAUSER-BMW MKM1000

THERE will always be a small number of motorcycle enthusiasts who insist on something different; it is their aim to improve upon excellence. If the prime mover is a German, he will pick on his native BMW as a candidate for the treatment. So it was with Mike Krauser, his name already famous for high quality, quickly detachable luggage systems. He looked at the top BMW of the time, the sporting R100RS, and found it wanting.

The first thing to go was the frame. Comfortable suspension and plenty of room for two had no place on the super-sporting machine he envisaged; nor did the rather simple (and inevitably flexible) tubular frame. Krauser commissioned German aircraft engineers to design an alternative, and they came up with a masterpiece of complexity, a veritable bird-cage of short straight tubes that double- and triple-triangulated one another for maximum rigidity.

The BMW suspension was modified to eliminate the mid-corner wallows, then the whole was clothed in compact bodywork that echoed the BMW's austere styling without the bulk; the petrol tank, seat and rear mudguard were unified in one piece of glass fibre.

Krauser then turned to the flat-twin engine. The overall design was excellent, well-balanced and well-cooled, but he wanted more flexibility as well as more urge at high revs. He commissioned a more modern four-valve head to replace the BMW's two valves, which not only improved the breathing throughout the rev range, but also lifted the rev ceiling.

The MKM1000 was a long time in the making, and all the careful development work has produced a fine bike. To ride, it is essentially a BMW – the familiar Boxer engine and the sensations of the shaft drive see to that. But it is a BMW apart.

First, there is the riding position, crouched over the bars in a sporting style. It throws the weight forward rather uncomfortably at lower speeds, but the more the wind lifts the rider, the better control becomes. The handling is concomitantly sporting, with a far more direct response to the subtleties of control than any standard BMW.

The engine modifications perform the same function of tautening up the German luxury bike to release its sporting potential. Curiously, the first sensation of the four-valve engine is of milder manners, since the Krauser pulls smoothly and strongly from below 3,000rpm. It is the crispness higher up the rev range that makes it a 130mph-plus machine.

The MKM1000 is exotic, very expensive, and very rare – a special version of a rather special breed.

KRAUSER-BMW MKM1000	
Engine	opposed twin, OHV four-valve
Cubic capacity	980cc
Maximum power	80bhp at 6250rpm
Bore × stroke	94 × 70.6mm
Gearbox	five-speed
Final drive	cardan shaft, crown-wheel-and-pinion
Wheelbase	54.4in
Dry weight	435lb
Top speed	139mph
Standing quarter mile	12.3sec
Date of launch	1982

MARTIN

FRANCE

RIGHT: *Moto Martin give their customers a choice of engines — anything goes, as long as its big, powerful and Japanese. Like the redoubtable big Kawasaki four, or the huge and high-revving Honda CBS Six (INSET).*

MOTO MARTIN

OTO Martin are a specialist chassis firm based in France and they manufacture their own frames, forks, wheels and bodywork. In addition they offer a comprehensive chassis conversion kit that will transform any large capacity Japanese motorcycle into an expensive and exclusive, highly-individual café racer. Their frames are all open loops featuring a huge, triangulated top section above the engine with flared top tubes that hug the motor's carburettors and cam covers. The engine itself completes the loop and is fully stressed. Any inline four or six cylinder lump of recent vintage can be used as a donor bike. From there on in, the full specification is entirely up to the buyer and the capacity of his wallet.

The Martin frame is made of chrome-moly tubing, neatly gas welded, nickel plated and considerably lighter than the original equipment steel double cradle. Their frames are very strong and together with large-diameter Martin forks, an aluminium swing-arm and either a De Carbon or White Power monoshock, handling and roadholding become guaranteed qualities. What is on sale are the best after-market chassis components around. A typical Martin conversion will knock 100lb off the standard weight and have a shorter wheelbase and faster steering geometry. The result is a bike that knows nothing of wallowing, weaving, wobbling or frame flex.

Moto Martin have long made their name and reputation through attention to detail and unadulterated flash looks. All of their kits feature needle roller swing-arms, fork sliders and yokes in forged aluminium, taper roller steering bearings, quality clip-ons, rearsets, a tidy electrical harness and lovely controls and linkages – and everything is rose-jointed and anodized. The frame is designed to accept a massive six gallon endurance style gas tank plus a variety of Martin fairings and seat/tail units.

Stunning to look at, Moto Martin have found a unique niche in the market – a way of transforming wonderfully powerful Jap engines that come with weedy and heavy standard frames into something much more light, nimble and responsive. Engines can be left as stock or tuned since everything is at the discretion of the buyer. The basic investment is just a frame but the full specification guarantees a highly individual sports motorcycle. A two-wheeled, high-profile, high-roller.

Various options exist to fit any 750, 900 or 1100cc Japanese transverse four or six cylinder engine. All Moto Martin conversions feature an open loop cantilever frame made of 25CD45 chrome moly tubing, gas welded and nickel plated.

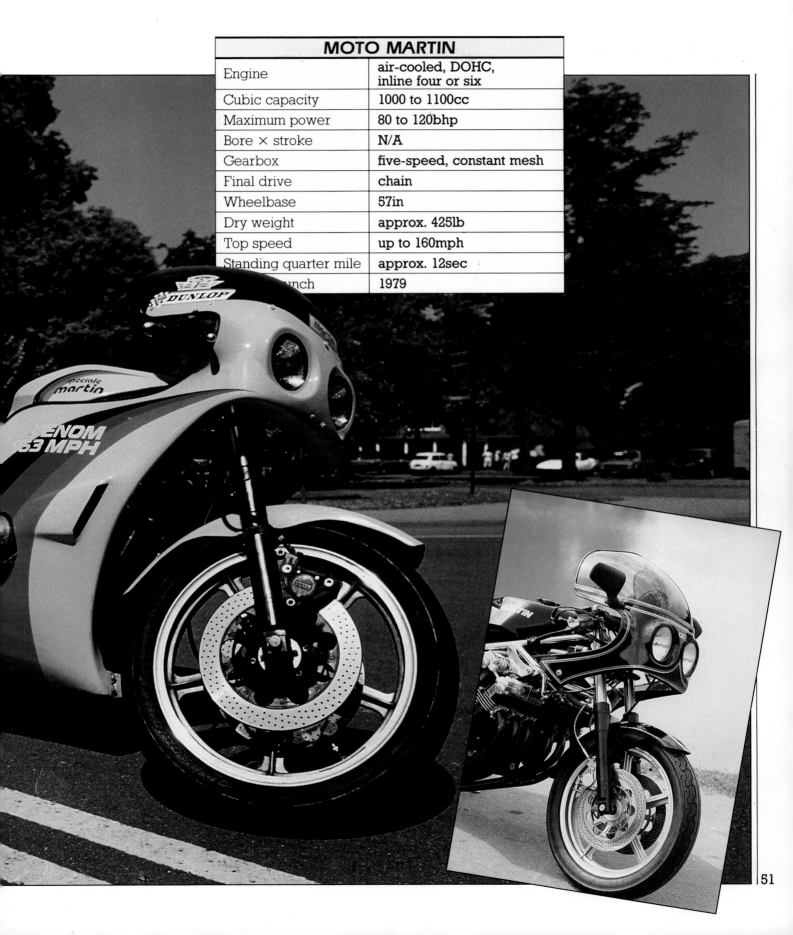

MOTO MARTIN

Engine	air-cooled, DOHC, inline four or six
Cubic capacity	1000 to 1100cc
Maximum power	80 to 120bhp
Bore × stroke	N/A
Gearbox	five-speed, constant mesh
Final drive	chain
Wheelbase	57in
Dry weight	approx. 425lb
Top speed	up to 160mph
Standing quarter mile	approx. 12sec
unch	1979

HARLEY-DAVIDSON

USA

RIGHT: *The classic sporting Harley, the XLCR (pronounced Excelsior) was lean, black, and thundrous — a throbbing, shaking live animal of a motorcycle. Venerable design kept it below the outer limits of superbike speed, but phenomenal low-rev and mid-range torque earned it a special place in the hall of fame.*

HARLEY-DAVIDSON XLCR

THE Harley Davidson XLCR is known in the heart of every red-blooded motorcyclist around the world as a dream café racer – mean, moody, magnificent and *very* black. It is known by many names – Big Black, Black Knight, the Black Brute, Rolling Thunder and plain old XLCR (pronounced Excelsior – how else?) With a black fairing, black cylinders, black cases and black pipes, it looks, sounds and smells like a mighty motorcycle, and it is, caviar on wheels.

Big Black is the fastest production bike Harley-Davidson have ever built. On skyscraper-tall gearing, it hits a good 120mph absolutely flat out. If top speed alone were the criterion for inclusion in this book, no Harley would make the grade. Any current Japanese 550cc machine will knock the pants off it in acceleration, roll-on and top speed tests, but this is to miss the point. The XLCR is about a different kind of power – the biggest V-twin around with extraordinarily long-stroking thumping power. You can count the power pulses at low revs when it rocks rather than vibrates. Two massive 81mm pistons are undertaking a long 96.8mm journey on every stroke and the 9:1 compression ratio helps them on their way with an almighty bang. The XLCR is about a different kind of image – low, massive and mean. Purposeful, powerful, delectable, it is a lean and shadowy beast with a road-shaking 1000cc V-twin lump. In fact, the XLCR is no more mythical than a race-modified Sportster 997cc engine in the smaller and lighter frame of Harley's XR750 flat-track racer. That, in conjunction with some stunning looks, is enough to make it the most desirable Harley ever.

At 520lb, it is fairly light for a Harley and it handles adroitly, all things considered. The novel siamesed exhausts give extra power but hardly maximum efficiency. Above all else, the bike has been tailored for looks. The casings are gargantuan and finished in crinkle-black. All of the paintwork and cycle gear is beautifully turned out. Light the fuse and it ticks over lazily but with the most profound bass note any four-stroke has ever produced. At full noise, the exhaust explosions are exquisite: a booming, deafening storm. Lovely. A Harley never barks (maximum torque is at 3800rpm, how could it?) It thumps – and how. Naturally it pulls like a train. The XLCR makes so much torque, it only needs a four-speed gearbox, nicely spaced and with a usefully tall top ratio. Vibration is awful – bad enough to undo the screws retaining major components at up to 80mph, smooth enough up to the ton and definitely on its own anywhere above. In its favour, it is *always* tractable, with power to go a-plenty.

HARLEY DAVIDSON XLCR	
Engine	air-cooled, OHV, 45 degree, V-twin
Cubic capacity	997.5cc
Maximum power	61bhp at 6200rpm
Bore × stroke	81 × 96.8mm
Gearbox	four-speed
Final drive	triplex chain
Wheelbase	58.5in
Dry weight	520lb
Top speed	120mph
Standing quarter mile	13.9sec
Date of launch	1976

Contradictions and creative legends surround all Harleys. They are exotic, evocative pieces of hardware, essentially unchanged since the dawn of motorcycling and all the better for it. Harley-Davidsons are all things to all people – raw, uncivilized and brutish; classic, owner-accessible and with a plain, no-nonsense image; last of the *real* motorcycles. To say their agricultural engine combines really usable power with good handling would not be enough. Never forget the look, the style, the desperado image and the fact that Harley-Davidson make *the* biggest V-twin motorcycles in the world.

The much more recent XR1000 street racer could be the quickest four-stroke, V-twin ever. Based on the XR750 engine, it sports aluminium heads and twin carbs, makes 70bhp at 5600rpm and runs the quarter mile in 12.7sec. Like the XLCR and all Harleys, it is a looker, and yes, it is finished in black.

HARRIS

RIGHT AND INSET: *High style, race-bred roadholding and plenty of Japanese power are the Harris ingredients for superlative road bikes. Typical of a small English firm that grew on the strength of reputation for quality, their latest Harris Magnum II is for the man who wants something better as well as different, and the ultimate specification is to his personal requirements.*

HARRIS MAGNUM

HARRIS Magnum is a highly individual, no compromise, top dog sports bike. It is individual because it is always up to the customer what level of specification he wants, uncompromising in that the Harris objective is fine handling and road-holding at speed, so comfort is strictly secondary. It is a top dog sports machine because ... well, look at the pictures. Dream machines are made like this. Harris Performance Products used to be a small, specialist chassis firm whose main interest was racing and frame/suspension development. Today they are Britain's largest bike manufacturers, a curious fact since they do not make any engines or offer much in the way of tuning gear except for their own four-into-one exhaust systems. Their main business is still in fine-tuning a rolling chassis.

Although they will endeavour to accommodate any engine, their name has been made using Kawasaki and Suzuki fours of all sizes (550 to 1100). They are still keenly involved in both two-stroke and four-stroke racing chassis but the various incarnations of the Magnum have all been for the road. All of them feature an open loop, monoshock frame, hand-made and taking a skilled welder around 30 hours to construct. They know nothing of mass-production and less still of assembly-line robots. The Magnum's fully-triangulated space frame uses the engine as a partially stressed member. None of the steel tubing is above the engine, instead there are widely-splayed steel tubes up top giving wide and strong support to the engine's sides and the steering head. The engine hangs below from the crankcases down, completing the open loop. The lightweight frame shows obvious hand-crafted touches. All the joints are fully profiled, bronze-welded and very clean to look at.

Having rehoused a Japanese powerplant in a strong and extremely rigid frame, it makes sense to kit it out with other redoubtable components. Harris make their own aluminium swing-arms and rocker arm linkages, including a rising-rate system. They prefer to use White Power rear units available in three specifications, all of them infinitely adjustable for spring preload. The most expensive has a remote gas reservoir with 11 rebound damping settings. Harris also advocate Marzocchi forks and painstakingly strip each pair to match them exactly. For wheels, they recommend Dymags with Brembo brakes.

Harris make their own excellent tanks and fairings plus all bodywork, mounts and linkages. The result is a supreme road bike. Typically it would be lower, lighter, smaller and more compact than the original donor bike,

HARRIS MAGNUM II	
Engine	air-cooled, DOHC, inline four
Cubic capacity	750 to 1100cc
Maximum power	70 to 120bhp
Bore × stroke	N/A
Gearbox	five-speed, constant mesh
Final drive	chain
Wheelbase	57.5in
Dry weight	approx. 425lb
Top speed	up to 160mph
Standing quarter mile	approx. 12sec
Date of launch	1983

say a Kawasaki or Suzuki 750 or 1100. The feel, however, is of something big and tall, a bit of a harsh handful around town, but definitely set up for speed work. On an open road, a Harris Magnum's roadholding, steering and handling are without equal. Everything just comes together, integrated and balanced, inspiring confidence and a heady turn of speed. It has taken ten years of single-minded horsepower development for the major manufacturers to wake up to the fact that their frames were rarely capable of nailing that horsepower to the ground. Today, with the outright power obsession fast receding, they are turning their attention to the twin problems of the cycle's weight and its chassis rigidity. Recently the major factories have been innovative and constructive but an enterprising firm like Harris has had the problem licked for years and the Japanese cannot compete. Harris are bespoke builders of motorcycles – their products are hand-made, labour-intensive and expensive. Where Harris do not manufacture a component, they advise the customer what to choose from the very best after-market accessories. Nothing comes at a premium on a Magnum, but then it has no peers. It is an aggressive-looking and performing, individually-assembled and quality-equipped sports bike for the discerning individual – the best of all possible worlds.

BRITAIN

RIGHT, CENTRE AND OPPOSITE RIGHT:
*Displaying a suitably
stiff upper lip nonchalance,
Lord Hesketh's Vampire
flies in the face of fashion,
with a look all of its
own. The intention was
to build a two-wheeled
Aston Martin, and there's
no doubt it's a bike that
puts the 'Grand' back into
Grand Touring'.*

HESKETH VAMPIRE

CONCEIVED by an English lord and built by British craftsmen in the tradition of the Vincent and the Brough Superior, the Hesketh is a natural aristocrat among modern motorcycles. Fittingly, perhaps, it is also extremely rare. The fully-faired Vampire version is the rarest of them all.

The enterprise was not planned that way. Originally, the motor-racing peer Lord Hesketh planned for series production rising to 100 per month, but the original bike ran into trouble with press criticism only weeks before production was due to begin, and its showroom debut had to be delayed for six months while a gearchange problem was solved.

When the production lines did start rolling, it was too late to save the company, and they went into liquidation after a year of difficulties. Lord Hesketh personally revived the machine, building them by hand in his castle stable yard; since then, production has moved to London, to a specialist firm called Mocheck.

The Hesketh ended up as many believed it should have begun – as an exclusive craftsman-built special, offering the best of British motorcycling tradition at a premium price.

That tradition includes many fine concepts of which one is accurate and dependable roadholding. There are some who find the Hesketh's steering a little ponderous, but there is no doubt that it sticks to its chosen line like glue.

Another is a high-quality frame, with noteworthy detail work that it takes a craftsman to perform. The Hesketh has a sturdy nickel-plated frame of straight tubes, using the engine and gearbox casing as a stressed member to mount the rear pivoted fork. The quality of the welding is plain to see.

A third is a relaxed engine with a deep exhaust note that delivers ample power and speed without ever sounding as though it is working hard. So it is with the Hesketh. The 1000cc engine has just two cylinders in a well-balanced 90 degree format. At low revs you can count the individual piston strokes; while four-valves per cylinder, a pair of overhead camshafts, and electronic ignition allow the flexible engine free reign to more than 6000rpm.

Every British motorcycle should be allowed a touch of eccentricity. Hesketh's is the full fairing for the Vampire. Painted an extraordinary metallic pink, it blends complete weather protection with an aerodynamic design that is partly futuristic and unique.

Although capable of well over 125mph, the Vampire is better loping along at 100mph, the engine throbbing gently, the fairing cutting a clean path through the wind.

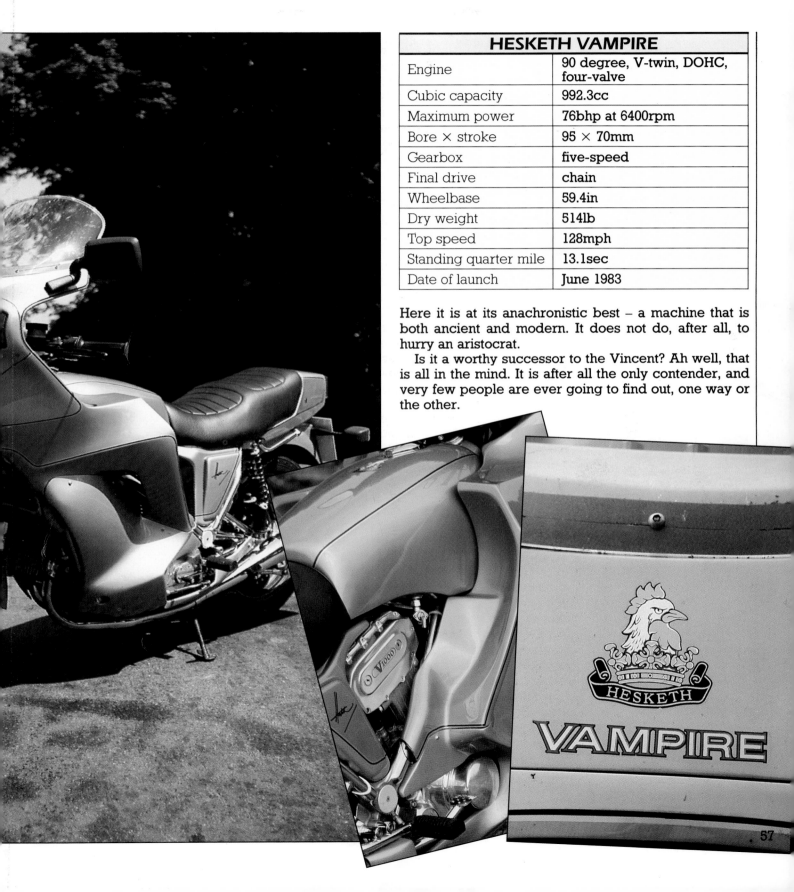

HESKETH VAMPIRE

Engine	90 degree, V-twin, DOHC, four-valve
Cubic capacity	992.3cc
Maximum power	76bhp at 6400rpm
Bore × stroke	95 × 70mm
Gearbox	five-speed
Final drive	chain
Wheelbase	59.4in
Dry weight	514lb
Top speed	128mph
Standing quarter mile	13.1sec
Date of launch	June 1983

Here it is at its anachronistic best – a machine that is both ancient and modern. It does not do, after all, to hurry an aristocrat.

Is it a worthy successor to the Vincent? Ah well, that is all in the mind. It is after all the only contender, and very few people are ever going to find out, one way or the other.

Norton

BRITAIN

RIGHT AND INSET: *As much legend as motorbike, the last of the expected mass of Wankel Rotary powered bikes has yet to see production. The bike is smooth, quiet, agile and fast — as a handful of privileged traffic offenders will attest. Note the air passage between the twin rotors — most other Wankels were water-cooled, and inevitably heavy.*

NORTON ROTARY

NOBODY could accuse Norton Motors of rushing the Rotary into production. It was to be the last product from a famous British motorcycling name. Prototypes were first shown to the press in the early 1970s. Fifteen years later, the bike had still not gone into production. It had, however, been steadily developed, and is in use by several police forces in Britain, who report on it favourably.

The delay was partly because of the troubles that afflicted Norton among all the great British bike factories; indeed, the Rotary was a project plucked from the collapsing empire to survive after the production lines had ceased forever. It was also partly due to the change in fortunes of the Wankel rotary motor. Once hailed as the engine of the future, its heralded takeover from the piston engine never came to pass. Instead, it became an orphan of the 1973 fuel crisis, dropped like a hot brick by the major car manufacturers.

Although developed at the same time as the car manufacturers' engine, Norton's rotary had always been rather different in detail. It is air-cooled, and oil-cooled, since jets of lubricant are directed internally to the rotors and the engine.

For years, the Norton Wankel stayed out of the limelight, while a small team covered thousands of road-test miles to iron out the flaws. By the mid-1980s, production was said (not for the first time) to be imminent, and the new Norton became not unfamiliar to persistent traffic regulation offenders. To most of us law-abiding citizens, however, it remained something of a legend.

The few people who have ridden one have all commented on the bike's tremendous flexibility, as well as an impressive turn of speed. The Wankel engine's prime asset is its wide range of power, together with an ability to rev freely without vibration or strain. Norton's achievement is to combine these properties in a unit shaped to fit well in a motorcycle frame.

True to Norton's tradition, that frame is a paragon of accurate steering and good roadholding. Quite conventional in its tubular construction and twin-shock rear suspension, the Norton has earned praise both from police riders and civilians for its good handling. From the police also come good reports of its reliability and longevity.

When will the new Norton go into series production? The question is impossible to answer. If you want to be sure of seeing one, break the speed limit in certain areas of central England. Sooner or later, you will hear the buzzing exhaust note, along with a wailing siren, and you will have discovered a Norton Rotary.

NORTON ROTARY	
Engine	Twin-rotor Wankel rotary
Cubic capacity	588cc nominal
Maximum power	84bhp at 9000rpm
Bore × stroke.	not applicable (compression ratio 8.5:1)
Gearbox	five-speed
Final drive	oil-bath chain
Wheelbase	59.5in
Dry weight	597lb in full police trim
Top speed	125mph (estimated)
Standing quarter mile	12.0sec (estimated)
Date of launch	not yet available

BRITAIN

RIGHT AND OPPOSITE BELOW RIGHT: *It may look like a plumber's nightmare, but the complex tubular frame and exhaust pipework to the turbocharger add up to the fastest-accelerating streetbike in Britain ... and that's official. Amazingly, owner Hunt also rides it to work!*

OPPOSITE ABOVE RIGHT: *The green bike is another Spondon with a Kawasaki engine, but no turbocharger.*

SPONDON TURBO GSX1100

IMAGINE a street-legal motorcycle capable of covering the standing quarter mile in less than ten seconds and breaking the finishing beams at more than 140mph, an ultimate street bike.

The Spondon Turbo GSX1100 is one such. It is not a production motorcycle but a fine example of how a stock Japanese bike can be turned into one of the fastest road-legal two-wheelers in the world. The bike belongs to English enthusiast Bill Hunter, who built and regularly races it in street class drag meets. He also rides it to work every day.

It is in no sense a new bike. At its heart is a 1980 Suzuki GSX1100 engine fitted with a Mr Turbo kit featuring a Rayjay turbo-charger, a single 38mm Keihin carburettor, a Facet fuel pump and a trick exhaust system with four equal length header pipes plus a single fat silencer. The motor has 1168cc Wiseco forged pistons, the biggest possible fit with standard liners, running 8:1 compression. The crank has been welded up, the cylinders honed, the standard size valves reground and the gears lightened and undercut. The cylinder head is from an 1100cc Katana. Add some slotted cam sprockets, alter the valve timing, give it 30 degrees of ignition advance and run some heavy-duty ignition components together with a very heavy-duty clutch and the result is a quarter mile rocketship capable of lifting the front wheel in fourth gear at 120mph.

The turbo comes in at 3,000rpm, boost pressure can be anywhere between 12 and 25psi, top speed is somewhere over the rainbow. The bike is geared for a theoretical 175mph. In truth, Bill does not know how fast it will go but he has a lot of fun trying to find out.

He used to run this fire-breathing, road-tearing engine in a stock GSX1100 chassis but it was not capable of containing that much power. Bill then approached Spondon Engineering, a small and specialist English chassis firm, who built him a one-off frame. It is an open cradle, a fortress of tubing, with a vertically mounted White Power shock at the rear and a unique box-section alloy swing-arm that allows a 4 inch variation in wheelbase and gives the option of running five different chain lengths. For the road, Bill runs a tight and short wheelbase. At the drag strip it gets the full extension for maximum traction. The front forks are standard but it sits on 18in Dymag magnesium wheels with Spondon magnesium dual piston calipers and discs. According to Bill, the chassis does everything: 'drag racing, road racing, touring ... you name it.'

Like all home-built, bolt-on turbo conversions, the bike gets through an awful lot of head gaskets, pistons, piston rings and gears. Fortunately it has been blessed

with a sound crankshaft and its proud, beaming owner is a speed-happy man. Only he knows how it feels to sail over the quarter mile finishing line at over 140mph. He says it is pure magic.

SPONDON TURBO GSX1100	
Engine	air-cooled, turbo-charged, DOHC, inline four
Cubic capacity	1168cc
Maximum power	approx. 135bhp at 10000rpm
Bore × stroke	75 × 66mm
Gearbox	five-speed, constant mesh
Final drive	sealed, roller chain
Wheelbase	58.5 to 62.5in variable
Dry weight	485lb
Top speed	175mph
Standing quarter mile	9.87sec
Date of launch	1980

RIGHT AND OPPOSITE BELOW RIGHT: *Race-style gear-driven camshafts are a key to the exotic level of equipment in Honda's 1000cc V4 flagship; the clever way they have silenced the gnashing gear-train (with secondary gears spring-loaded out of phase) is the key to how they have civilized it for the road. A bike for a dedicated specialist.*

HONDA VF1000R

THE VF1000R is Honda's flagship, the fastest and most powerful motorcycle they have ever made. It is a street-legal replica of the racer on which Ulsterman Joey Dunlop won the Formula One World Championship. Since that championship was held largely on public road circuits with real bumps, the bike is a very accurate copy. It is also very expensive. As befits any serious King of the Roads machine, it has an enormous amount of power. Honda's V4, four-stroke range (400, 500, 750 and 1000cc) is characterized by heavily oversquare, short-stroking engines. They are smooth yet hard-revving with a broad power band which combines thunderous acceleration with rivers of torque. The 1000R is Honda's biggest and best 90 degree, V4 engine not only because of its 122bhp output and 11,000rpm redline (very high for a bike of this capacity) but also because of one unique feature – it has gear driven camshafts.

The increased accuracy of valve timing available from gear driven cams has long been recognized in racing circles where precise, high rpm valve operation is crucial. Disadvantages include prohibitive manufacturing costs, weight and noise. Honda's camshaft gear train is undoubtedly heavier than chain drive, but it is surprisingly quiet. The extra tooling costs were of course passed on to the consumer. The engine performance is wonderful. There is plenty of low-down punch, fast response and fabulous acceleration. It can be short-shifted, just rolling on the torque or redlined through five gears to a genuine top speed of more than 150mph. The frame is a steel cradle with similarly conventional front and rear suspension. Everything on this bike is big and strong and it needs to be. Fully gassed (5.5gal) is weighs 620lb. Even so, it is stable right up to its top speed.

Handling and roadholding are good bearing in mind the weight and bulk of the bike. The steering is heavy despite a 16in front wheel shod with a fat 120 section tyre. The rear tyre is a radial, the first ever to be fitted to a production bike. Released initially in a limited edition, the VF1000R is a high-profile, head-turning, modern classic. Its racing pedigree, sheer class and stylish contours are brazenly displayed, enhanced by bold graphics and a feast of rich colours. It is both well-finished and stunning to look at. There are some lovely details as well: floating brake discs, a quickly detachable front wheel, a carbon-fibre reinforced fairing, braided steel brake lines and penetrating twin headlights. Is it the ultimate posing tool or a serious race bike? The answer is both. It is a bit *too* heavy and *too* big for many road riders. Only a professional racer could get the very

best out of it, flat out against the stop for any distance. Motorcycle connoisseurs around the world have complained of its top heavy feel and concluded it was not worth the considerably higher price compared to Honda's more standard VF1000F – a high-barred model with chain driven cams but otherwise an almost identical specification and level of performance.

HONDA VF1000R	
Engine	liquid-cooled, DOHC, 90 degree, V4
Cubic capacity	998cc
Maximum power	122bhp at 10,000rpm
Bore × stroke	77 × 53.6mm
Gearbox	five-speed, constant mesh
Final drive	sealed, roller chain
Wheelbase	59.3in
Dry weight	525lb
Top speed	155mph
Standing quarte	
Date of launch	

JAPAN

ABOVE AND BELOW RIGHT: *The NS400's resemblance to Honda's works grand prix racers is more than skin deep. Though the engine layout has been inverted to suit the street, the aluminium frame, anti-dive suspension, lightweight wheels and low-drag body are just like the real thing. Front wheel high, works rider Ron Haslam demonstrates.*

HONDA NS400

IN 1983 Freddie Spencer, riding for Honda, became the youngest 500cc World Champion ever. Two years later, in belated celebration, Honda released the NS400, a bike claimed to be a road-going replica of Spencer's machine. The result is a fast, small, very light, two-stroke sports bike, beautifully finished with quite outstanding handling and road-holding. It may be 100cc smaller and considerably less powerful than the brutal all-or-nothing factory racer but they genuinely do have enough in common to warrant the Grand Prix replica tag. Like the racer, the NS400 is a liquid-cooled, three cylinder two-stroke of an unusual configuration, a V3. The outer pair of cylinders are arranged forwards and down with a vertical middle cylinder. It is a light, narrow unit, no wider than a parallel twin. The 90 degree, V3 layout allows the chassis to be kept extremely compact. Mounted in a lightweight aluminium box-section frame, the engine weight is low and carried forward to give a good centre of gravity. The carburettors are carefully arranged inside the V to keep the engine short, hence the wheelbase can be kept short too. Weighing only 359lb with a 54.5in wheelbase, the NS is the lightest and quickest bike in its class. It is fast, nimble and responsive. You can change lines on it as quickly as on a genuine racer.

Unlike many sporting two-strokes, the power the NS makes is not that peaky or rough. Honda use their own version of an exhaust power valve called ATAC (auto-controlled torque amplification chambers) on the front two cylinders to help the power spread at low revs. Even so there is little or no acceleration below 5,000rpm but there is a gradual build up between 5,000 and 7,000rpm, at which point it starts accelerating Ike crazy, screaming revs all the way to the redline. Surprisingly, it does this smoothly. If any two-stroke can be said to have manners, then the NS has more than most.

Peak power is at 10,000rpm, and it falls away immediately afterwards. Kept on the boil between 7,000 and 10,000rpm through six close gears, it is an indecently quick bike. Anywhere between 50 and 110mph, typically piling on the speed out of a corner, it will embarrass even 1000cc machines with the sheer fury of its acceleration.

There is no point in having a 130mph 400 unless you can regularly use all the performance, nailing the power to the ground with confidence. Fortunately, Honda have designed the perfect rolling chassis for their potent motor.

On road or track, the handling is always sharp and precise. The steering is quick and comfortable and the bike has excellent brakes. The only limit to its road-

holding seems to be the edge of the tyres. While other two-strokes display hesitant, unconfident handling with the power often being snappy, vicious and unsettling, the little Honda is an integrated, professional sports machine. Beautiful to look at and dazzling in performance, the NS400 is a worthy replica of a championship-winning bike. The worst thing you can say about it is that it is a shame they did not make it a 500. As it is, the NS is exciting and pretty near faultless.

HONDA NS400	
Engine	liquid-cooled, 90 degree, V3, two-stroke
Cubic capacity	387cc
Maximum power	72bhp at 10,000rpm
Bore × stroke	57 × 50.6mm
Gearbox	six-speed, constant mesh
Final drive	sealed, roller chain
Wheelbase	54.5in
Dry weight	359lb
Top speed	135mph
Standing quarter mile	12.1sec
	1985

HONDA

JAPAN

RIGHT AND OPPOSITE BELOW RIGHT: *Latest, maybe last, in a line of across-the-frame fours directly descended from Honda's first superbike, the swift CBX exhibits steady progress. The power unit is more compact, more powerful, and maybe more civilized; the bike handles much better, and goes 20mph faster. Amazingly, 15 years have also made the engine design seem relatively simple, compared with the later water-cooled machines.*

HONDA CBX750

THE CBX750 could well be Honda's last offering in the classic, inline four cylinder 750 family. The factory are now firmly committed to V4 engines powering their large sports bike and the future for any large, air-cooled, inline engine is uncertain.

The release of the CBX marked the end of 15 years of uninterrupted CB750/4 production, involving countless revisions, new engines and updates. Honda were the first to launch an inline 750/4 – the original superbike – back in 1969. It used a SOHC, eight valve engine and produced 67bhp. For comparison, the CBX750 features a DOHC, 16 valve engine and produces 91bhp.

The CBX differs from its many predecessors in some significant ways. The top end of the motor is remarkable for employing hydraulic tappets, hardly a new idea (Harley-Davidson have used them for decades) but unique on a Japanese production motorcycle. The advantage to the owner in not having to set 16 valve clearances is obvious. Honda have added thin-stemmed lightweight valves making for less reciprocating weight.

Weight saving and compact design are in evidence everywhere on the engine. Its width was reduced by placing the big 320W alternator behind the cylinders instead of spinning on the crank end. Height was reduced by making the sump shallower and redeploying the front frame tubes as oil carriers, a novel redistribution that actually increases the total oil capacity. Finally, Honda pruned the engine length by dispensing with the jackshaft between crank and clutch. Primary drive is by direct gear from the crank; one of the crank webs has been turned into a gear pinion.

Engine performance is marked by smoothness and excellent tractability. The CBX makes good low-down power aided by some low gearing. The mid-range is a bit flat and lacks snap but acceleration is very healthy at the top end, above 8,000rpm. The bike is so smooth and uncannily quiet at speed that Honda deemed it necessary to fit a rev limiter that cuts in at 10,800rpm.

The engine's compactness means that it can be mounted lower in the frame, partially compensating for its inherent top heaviness. The steering is very quick, and handling and roadholding are exceptionally good for a bike of this size and weight.

The CBX is genuinely flickable, largely because of its low frontal area and careful weight distribution (48.6/ 51.4 front and rear). It is stable up to top speed though the smart and sleek half-fairing is more of a sports cockpit than a touring windcheater. The dual headlights are a bonus for any road user, 120W of sharp illumination on dip or main beams.

Although the release of the CBX750 marks the end of Honda's development of inline engines, the bike is a shade quicker and more powerful than the V4 VF750 which was also released early in 1984. The second generation V4 750, the VFR750F, is based on Honda's successful endurance race bike. It has gear driven cams and makes 105bhp at 11,000rpm. Development and progress go on as ever, but will they still be making V4 750s in 15 years time?

HONDA CBX750

Engine	air-cooled, DOHC, inline four
Cubic capacity	747cc
Maximum power	91bhp at 9500rpm
Bore × stroke	67 × 53mm
Gearbox	six-speed, constant mesh
Final drive	sealed, roller chain
Wheelbase	57.7in
Dry weight	480lb
Top speed	137mph
Standing quarter mile	11.9sec
Date of launch	1984

HONDA ASPENCADE GL1200

N the move, it is not the size of the Aspencade that is the most obvious thing. It is the smooth and fluid engine; its capability of running at well over the ton for mile after mile, never straining, always comfortable, and never, ever, feeling short of power.

Honda's Gold Wing of the mid-1970s started big and kept getting bigger. In its original form it was an unfaired machine, and the liquid-cooled flat four engine displaced 1000cc. At that time, nobody had seen anything quite so enormous.

It was not long before the luxury touring riders of the USA started fitting out their Gold Wings for the long haul down Easy Street. Their requirements gave birth to an accessory industry supplying everything from super-soft 'King and Queen' seats to gigantic fairings with matching three-piece luggage equipment, as well as air suspension to smooth the ride to the standards of a family car.

The Aspencade (named after the biggest gathering of touring riders in the USA) was Honda's answer. It was as if to say: 'Anything you can, we can do better.' They meant it. The Aspencade comes equipped with *everything*. With panniers and a gigantic top box, you can carry luggage enough for three. Want to take the barbecue? Load it right on.

The massive fairing not only offers complete weather protection, it is also built to the very highest standards, with plenty of lock-up storage compartments, and a ventilation system. It is possible to order a stereophonic radio and tape player as well, to add music to the passing zephyr. The engine certainly makes no noise loud enough to drown it, though you should not use the Aspencade's considerable speed potential if you want to hear the high notes.

To cope with the sort of loads an Aspencade rider might wish to carry, Honda installed their own air suspension – with an extra refinement. An on-board compressor is built into the bike, and the springing can be made harder or softer without even stopping; firming the ride up for more stability when swinging through the mountain bends, and then softening it to a lulling wallow on the long straights through the deserts. Of course, the gross tonnage of the Aspencade is not to everybody's taste. This tourer supreme is a specialist vehicle, just as much as a race-replica Ducati, but in a different way.

Honda overcame the weight by expanding the engine to 1200cc, broadening the spread of the power as well as adding to peak performance. The Aspencade retains a healthy acceleration from low to high speeds, as well as an ability to cruise relatively econo-

mically in a tall top gear. With shaft drive and that big, lazy engine, maintenance is an infrequent chore. The Aspencade was developed with long distances as well as high speeds in mind. It will keep on running as long as its pampered and cossetted rider wants it to.

It was designed for the US roads and is as American as a Japanese bike can be. Honda get round proposed or actual import restrictions by assembling the Aspencade in their US factory. Honda's new machine has spawned imitators from the Japanese rivals. But Honda did it first, and the bike is still the definitive heavyweight luxury tourer.

HONDA ASPENCADE GL1200	
Engine	liquid-cooled, SOHC, opposed four
Cubic capacity	1182cc
Maximum power	93bhp at 7000rpm
Bore × stroke	75.5 × 66mm
Gearbox	five-speed, constant mesh
Final drive	shaft
Wheelbase	63.4in
Dry weight	720lb
	119mph
	13.2sec
	1983

JAPAN

RIGHT AND INSET: Candidate for 'Fastest Bike On The Planet' title, Kawasaki's 160 plus mph GPZ1000R explored new frame technology, and new levels of refined but excessive horsepower. Too much of a good thing?

T was inevitable that the horsepower wars would have to end at some stage. For over 15 years, the Japanese manufacturers have been locked in a battle with each other to produce motorcycle ultimates; a never-ending race to build quicker, faster, more powerful super bikes. A race in where there could never be an outright winner and the only certain loser was motorcycling itself. The GPz1000R marks Kawasaki's voluntary retirement from that race. They say they will never build a quicker bike – 125bhp and 162mph is the ceiling on speed and power output that Kawasaki have adopted, while the avowed aim of this, their swan-song, is a flagship that will 'outperform competing 1000cc-plus sportsbikes for some years'.

Certainly the GPz1000R is one of the two candidates for the title of the fastest road bike on the planet (the other is Suzuki's GSX-R1100). Over the years, as the mass-produced superbike has progressed, it has been increasingly possible to attain regularly (and illegally) a speed of 130 or 140mph. Recently, there have been plenty of bikes (750s included) capable of nearly 150mph. What can be the fate of 160mph motorcycles other than eventual extinction at the hands of governments and interfering legislators? Kawasaki at least, have been brave – and realistic – enough to throw down the gauntlet for the last time. The GPz1000R is a magnificent beast of a motorcycle. How could it possibly be otherwise? It has performance unlimited.

At its heart is a bored and stroked version of their award-winning GPz900R engine, a liquid-cooled, DOHC, 16 valve, transverse four, as technologically advanced and sophisticated as any lump around. Having decided on one last mega-bike, a horsepower-packed speedball, their engine designers looked at all the possible types of engine configuration from V4s and V6s to straight sixes; they concluded, nevertheless, that their tried and trusted inline four was still the best, and one that Kawasaki have stuck with since the heady, halcyon days of the 1970s and the Z1.

The 1000R has more power everywhere than the 900 but also more bulk and weight. The engine has been rubber mounted because of increased vibration but otherwise it follows the same careful and compact pattern – wet liners, a cam chain repositioned at the side of the engine with the alternator above the gearbox. Features unique to the 1000R's dazzling engine specification include flat aluminium pistons, a unique cool air induction system and hand-polished intake ports. Surprisingly, it is not at all peaky. Power is available with a beautifully smooth surge from 3,000rpm and above 6,000rpm there is plain, no nonsense stomp all

the way to the 10,500rpm redline. Response is lively, strong and clean. This is not an engine for the faint-hearted.

Unlike the 900 which has a steel diamond frame using the engine as a stressed member, the 1000R gets an all new perimeter-type frame with square-section top rails curving wide around the engine to meet in a massively braced and extremely rigid steering head. Kawasaki claim the rear aluminium swing-arm is the strongest they have ever produced. There is state of the art suspension; Uni-Trak at the back with all the linkages placed below the single shock to keep the weight low. The 40mm braced forks with AVDS (automatic variable damping system) vary the compression damping according to changes in both the speed and distance of wheel travel. Wheels are 16in front and back, with low-profile tyres, the rear being a notable, drag strip like, 150/80 section.

Handling and roadholding are more than respectable for the weight and sheer size of the bike. Although it is undeniably more powerful and faster than its illustrious predecessor, the 900R, motorcycle enthusiasts around the world have also found it more cumbersome and unstable. The 900R is quicker through most bends and around a race-track because it is more manageable. Hence popular opinion has deemed the 1000R to be for professional use only and to rate the 900 as both a better all-rounder and a specifically better sports bike. One has even so to admit the 1000R's impressive specification and totally irresistible performance. It's just that maybe, after all, you *can* have too much of a good thing.

KAWASAKI GPz1000R	
Engine	liquid-cooled, DOHC, inline four
Cubic capacity	997cc
Maximum power	125bhp at 9500rpm
Bore × stroke	74 × 58mm
Gearbox	six-speed, constant mesh
Final drive	sealed, roller chain
Wheelbase	59.3in
Dry weight	525lb
Top speed	162mph
Standing quarter mile	10.6sec
Date of launch	1985

Kawasaki

RIGHT: *The six-cylinder king of Kawasaki's jungle is more elephant than lion, with all the massive size and effortless power that implies. In fact, smaller-engined supersports models are faster in every way, but nothing can rival the impassive way the biggest (and last) of the Japanese sixes hums quietly to absurdly illegal speeds. Handling is surprisingly light ... unless it falls off its stand, and you have to lift it up. A likeable monster.*

KAWASAKI Z1300

THE Z1300, although it was not the first six-cylinder motorcycle, is the biggest and the longest-lived. Its hallmark is calm, unruffled high performance, with a silky-smooth engine. If at first it seemed impossibly large and heavy, the others have now caught up and it no longer seems so out of place.

The Z1300 is a trend-setter in a number of respects apart from sheer size. It was an early pioneer of liquid cooling, which has since become common practice. It was one of the first bikes which sacrificed the ultimate power of a really big engine in favour of a soft-spoken spread of power that was more akin to a large luxury car. Given the size of the engine there was still plenty left for astoundingly high performance.

In the second series of the Z1300, Kawasaki introduced electronic fuel injection, which they had perfected on the more sporting GPz1100. This brought new levels of refinement as well as improved economy and extra power. The injection is instantly noticeable, simply because it makes the quiet, smooth engine so completely unobtrusive. It will start on the merest touch of the button even if the motorcycle is covered with ice, and settle quickly to an even purring idle. Be warned, the bike is rather a daunting proposition actually to *ride* in such difficult conditions.

The roadholding is competent, given the bike's huge bulk and weight approaching 700lb. It is not the sort of bike to take liberties with on a wet road; when it does go out of control, there is an awful lot of metal to get back in line. In essence, and in spite of its complication, the Z1300 is a conventional motorcycle in everything except scale. The frame is a normal tubular steel item, the front forks are standard-issue telescopic, the rear is suspended with a rising-rate linkage.

The clutch that transmits the massive horsepower is a conventional multi-plate wet model, and the five-speed gearbox is slick-changing and betrays no overt sign of its obviously robust components. Wisely, Kawasaki chose shaft final drive. A normal motorcycle chain would not last long as the final link between such power and weight.

With 130 horsepower on tap, coupled with smooth mid-range power, the Z1300 is at its absolute best as a touring tug. It has more than enough power to push an enormous fairing through the wind and to carry as much luggage as can be fitted.

As a large-scale technical *tour-de-force*, the Z1300 has few rivals. However, Kawasaki chose to give it understated slab-sided styling, and offer it in sombre colours. It is well able to make its presence felt without over-the-top styling.

KAWASAKI Z1300	
Engine	liquid-cooled, DOHC, inline six
Cubic capacity	1286cc
Maximum power	130bhp at 7500rpm
Bore × stroke	62 × 71mm
Gearbox	five-speed, constant mesh
Final drive	shaft
Wheelbase	62.2in
Dry weight	648lb
Top speed	142mph
Standing quarter mile	11.6sec
Date of launch	1979

JAPAN

RIGHT AND OPPOSITE BELOW RIGHT: *Most successful and longest lived of the production turbo bikes, Kawasaki's Z750 solved the problems better than the rest, to give an instantly accessible boost to performance. The giant-killer promise of the turbo-charger at last came true.*

KAWASAKI Z750 TURBO

KAWASAKI were the last of the four major Japanese manufacturers to release a turbo-charged motorcycle but were the only factory to achieve the ultimate turbo ambition – to transform a medium-sized motorcycle into something as quick as anything around. The Z750 is the world's fastest production turbo motorcycle – 112bhp at 9,000rpm, a top speed of 146mph and road-tearing acceleration that can cover the standing quarter mile in 10.9sec.

For many years, turbo-charged bikes had been the preserve of individual builders, tuners and drag racers, who adapted big Japanese four cylinder engines with bolt-on conversions for extra, high-speed thrills. Later Honda, Suzuki and Yamaha produced turbo bikes, all 650cc and all dismally received in the market. Kawasaki's 750 was bigger yet lighter than any and an instant, well-acclaimed success. The others have all been withdrawn, but the Z750 still occupies a unique place in Kawasaki's sports bike range and enhances yet further their reputation for building large, powerful, bulletproof engines. On full boost, the Z750 Turbo shoots, shouts and screams speed.

Where Kawasaki significantly differed from the other manufacturers was in the design and location of their turbo-charger unit. They beefed up one of their existing inline four cylinder engines, the Z750, but instead of mounting the turbo behind the engine, Kawasaki put it up in front of the cylinders, very close to the exhaust ports. In a limited space of 7.5in, they managed to run four highly heat resistant steel pipes from the ports to a collector and thence to a tiny Hitachi turbo-charger. Such innovative positioning reduced turbo lag significantly. The result is instant response. Running a fairly modest 10.5psi of boost pressure the Z750 has excellent pick-up and strong acceleration anywhere above 5,000rpm when the turbo is spinning hard.

The turbo power does not bang in at a set rpm like many back street, bolt-on turbo bikes. From 5,000 to the 10,000rpm redline, there is plenty of boost and real poke, yet it is smoothly delivered. The turbo effect is unobtrusive. The acceleration is unforgettable.

In roll-on tests in high gears, the Kawasaki will annihilate much larger capacity bikes including its own big brother, the mighty GPz1000. The smooth response and excellently rounded power curve are helped considerably by Kawasaki's digital fuel injection system. Kawasaki pioneered fuel injection on modern sports bikes and their computer-linked system, measuring and monitoring engine speed, throttle opening, intake pressure and engine/air temperature, ensures the Turbo runs at its best. The rolling chassis is unremarkable but

for the sleek, full fairing which features an integrated, aluminium frame member. This is a central section located between the frame's front down tubes which makes the double steel cradle more rigid, improving stability and protecting the turbo unit from crash damage. One notable detail can be found in the sealed, O-ring, final drive chain which is silicone lubricated and has special cut-outs in every other link to reduce weight and heat build-up.

KAWASAKI Z750 TURBO	
Engine	air-cooled, turbo-charged, DOHC, inline four
Cubic capacity	738cc
Maximum power	112bhp at 9000rpm
Bore × stroke	66 × 54mm
Gearbox	five-speed, constant mesh
Final drive	sealed, roller chain
Wheelbase	58.7in
Dry weight	514lb
Top speed	146mph
Standing quarter mile	10.9sec
Date of launch	1983

SUZUKI

JAPAN

SUZUKI RG500 GAMMA

SUZUKI have been developing and refining a square four, two-stroke motorcycle for years. Since 1976 they have had at least one new model for every year but none of them was for sale. They were the exclusive property of the paid factory riders and were all works race bikes. Barry Sheene won the 1976 and 1977 500cc World Championships on an RG500. So did Marco Lucchinelli in 1981 and Franco Uncini in 1982. At the highest level of competition, the blue riband 500cc Grand Prix, Suzuki's RG has always been a fierce and formidable contender.

In 1985, Suzuki unveiled a stunning, spellbinding RG500 Gamma for the road. One might describe it as an authentic racer with lights. The race replica wars have certainly come a long way: replicas are now arguably as fast as some of the original racers on which they are based. Like the racing Gamma's, the street-legal RG is a liquid-cooled, twin crank, square four with disc valve induction. Fed by four ultra-thin, 28mm flat slide Mikuni carburettors located on the outside of each cylinder, and with the gas helped by Suzuki's intake power chamber on the way in and their power valve on the way out, the Gamma revs way beyond the redline and makes power in huge peaks of blistering stomp. There is little below 6,000rpm but it revs hard and fast to 9,000 where it starts falling away but then at 9,500rpm it is suddenly back on the pipe and *bang*, it revs wildly and is making horsepower up to 12,000rpm. Acceleration is mind-bending. Whacking open the throttle has those four tiny, delicate carburettors dancing at the end of their cables and cracking instantly into life. Run flat out through six well-spaced gears, it is *still* accelerating at 135mph and 9,500rpm in top.

Despite its peaky rev-craziness, the engine is not animal-like in behaviour and response. It is possible to drop below 6,000rpm without it dying or oiling up the plugs. The power is progressive and fairly smooth for a two-stroke.

At 340lb the Gamma is remarkably light for its size but it is also fairly tall. The alloy double cradle frame and full floater monoshock suspension do a fine job of keeping the wheels on the ground. The steering is not just quick but fast. It needs a positive, deliberate riding style but the reward is razor-sharp handling and beautiful roadholding. In order to reduce speed quickly the bike has very powerful brakes – twin 260mm front discs with four pot calipers that used hard will tear the rubber off the 16in front tyre.

The release of the RG500 poses an interesting question. Mechanically, the bike is very closely related to the legendary RG racer. Would a suitably prepared

version of the road bike have been capable of winning a 500cc GP race in the late 1970s? Who knows? The detail work on the RG is of such a high and exotic standard that it can only have been learnt from Suzuki's many years of developing and campaigning their factory racers. That is over ten years of racing secrets made available for the road. Blessed with an immaculate pedigree and a reputation forged on the racetracks of the world, the Gamma is an extremely fast and mighty projectile. Excitement guaranteed.

SUZUKI RG500 GAMMA	
Engine	liquid-cooled, square four, two-stroke
Cubic capacity	498cc
Maximum power	95bhp at 9500rpm
Bore × stroke	56 × 50mm
Gearbox	six-speed, constant mesh
Final drive	sealed, roller chain
Wheelbase	56.1in
Dry weight	340lb
Top speed	143mph
Standing quarter mile	11sec
Date of launch	1985

$ SUZUKI

RIGHT AND INSET: *The Suzuki GSX-R750 brings the racer-with-lights formula bang up to date — a companion model (without the lights) is race-ready straight out of the box. The engine is peaky, but 150mph from a 'mere' 750 does demand a few compromises.*

SUZUKI GSX-R750

T would be unfair to describe the GSX-R750 as a replica race bike for one simple reason – it *is* a race bike in the thinnest possible disguise. It is an out-of-the-crate racer, a works replica that was released both to the public and the serious professional at the same time, before the event instead of after it. During its first year on the market, the GSX-R won several important races and championships and nobody, from road rider to World Endurance or Formula One pilot, complained about its level of performance or competitiveness. Suzuki call it a Hyper-Sports machine, meaning that it is above, over, or in excess of, what would normally be expected from a 750cc motorcycle.

The GSX-R is an extraordinary bike for two main reasons. Firstly, it is an aggressive, business-like, no compromise, thoroughbred race tool. Secondly, it is extremely light, weighing 100lb less than its nearest 750 competitor – it is as light as Suzuki's own inline four 400. For these features alone, many consider the GSX-R to be the most significant motorcycle currently available, it will probably change the face and shape of future sports bikes. Those to come will have to be similarly light in order to be competitive. The Suzuki has set a very high standard and is a difficult act to follow. It represents the leading edge of motorcycle design and technology. 'Racing improves the breed' is no longer enough. Now it is 'Born on the circuit, returned to the circuit.' Hyper-Sports indeed.

Suzuki's remarkable weight-saving operation begins with the powerplant. The engine is an oversquare and very short-stroking, large valve, radically timed, humpy-cammed and high compression unit developing over 100bhp. Air cooling was clearly inadequate. Liquid cooling would have been the normal method to choose but Suzuki rejected it as adding unnecessarily to the weight and instead decided on oil cooling, a technique inspired by Second World War P51 Mustang fighter aircraft but unique among modern motorcycles.

The GSX-R uses the Suzuki Advanced Cooling System (SACS), a large oil cooler and two pumps which circulate and spray high volumes of lubricating oil through special tubes, passageways and galleries to the hot spots of the engine, for example above the combustion chambers and on the underside of the piston crowns. The oil cooler is larger than normal to cope with the increased capacity and the external cylinder cooling fins are much more densely arranged than on their other bikes.

Everything on the engine has been lightened – the crank, pistons, con rods, side covers, the four-into-one

exhaust system . . . everything. The cylinder head cover is made of magnesium, an expensive feature which saves 4lb over a conventional item. All in, engine weight is down by over 35lb compared to a water-cooled 750/4.

Naturally, Suzuki extended their severe weight saving plan to the chassis. The bare frame is in box-section aluminium and weighs only 18lb, approximately half the weight of a steel cradle. The rest of the chassis reflects racing needs – harsh, heavy duty suspension, 18in wheels front and back, and a Deca piston braking system, 10 pistons for three 300mm discs, four each up front and two for the rear. Add a full race fairing with twin halogen headlights and the dry weight totals 388lb or about 20 per cent less than an average four cylinder 750. The riding position is pure racer's crouch, low bars, high pegs and a long reach across the broad back of the tank. It can be banked to 55 degrees and will slam through bends, chicanes and all manner of corners without weave or wobble.

The GSX-R is a demanding and difficult bike to ride fast. There is little power below 6,000rpm and it is not at all torquey. It is a high rpm motor that comes into its own above 100mph. The throttle is stiff thanks to the flat slide carburettors. It is noisy – a really crisp bark explodes from the pipe. There are no soft edges, everything about the bike is hard and stiff yet sharp and precise. No compromise can be asked for or given, this is an out and out race bike for the road.

For 1986, Suzuki unleashed an 1100cc version of the GSX-R, a bored and stroked 130bhp monster that weighs only 434lb. It is the lightest ever and capable of 162mph which makes it a prime candidate for the fast-est bike in the world. Suzuki say they will never build a quicker bike.

SUZUKI GSX-R750	
Engine	liquid-cooled, DOHC, inline four
Cubic capacity	749cc
Maximum power	100bhp at 10,500rpm
Bore × stroke	70 × 48.7mm
Gearbox	six-speed, constant mesh
Final drive	sealed, roller chain
Wheelbase	56.5in
Dry weight	388lb
Top speed	150mph
Standing quarter mile	11.4sec
Date of launch	1985

YAMAHA

JAPAN

RIGHT AND INSET: *At ease among the real racers, Yamaha's two-stroke V4 500 was the first of the grand-prix replicas — based closely on the bike that won a world championship in 1984 for Eddie Lawson. It is a demanding bike to ride, if you wish to use all of its potential, but once mastered, it is possibly the fastest bike of all point-to-point on a twisty road.*

YAMAHA RD500LC

YAMAHA were the first of the major manufacturers to offer a genuine, two-stroke Grand Prix replica. The RD500LC was announced, rather prematurely, late in 1983 and caused a sensational amount of interest and anticipation. It looked like the most exciting motorcycle of the decade and it was – the fastest, most powerful, road-going 500 ever built with a specification that directly paralleled the factory racer used by Kenny Roberts to win six World Championship GP. It was a fearsome proposition and proved irresistible to enthusiasts everywhere.

The RD500LC was initially released in a strictly allocated limited edition but was sold out months in advance of its official release. When it was finally uncrated, nobody was disappointed. It started winning open class races immediately. The electrifying reputation that had preceded it was more than justified. Yamaha have long led the world in two-stroke development and as a factory have been involved in GP road racing for longer and with more success than anybody else. They have always made both factory racers for their works riders *and* production racers for aspiring individuals. The V4 500 was a fairly new design introduced in 1982 after years of campaigning, revising and refining the transverse four cylinder, two-stroke racer. Their claim that the RD500 was developed, tested and approved by Kenny Roberts and only deviates from the works racer with respect to improvements made to enhance the RD500 as a road bike, is no idle boast.

The LC is excitement personified – fast and light, nimble and responsive, excellent handling combined with some of the meanest, most ferocious power imaginable.

The engine is a very highly tuned 50 degree, V4 with the diagonally opposed cylinders firing simultaneously. It is basically two twin cylinder engines mated together – there are two cranks geared together with a balance shaft to smooth out the inevitable vibration. The motor is odd. Although each cylinder uses identical reed valves, the rear pair of pots have the reed block in the inlet tract and are piston ported while the front pair have the reed valves sitting directly in the crankcase. Each pair of cylinders gets one Yamaha power valve system unit, which rotates to vary the exhaust port timing throughout the rev range. Generally, the exhaust port timing is so radical that a real 500cc GP machine would not have been equipped with it a few years back.

The power it produces is not surprisingly, peaky. The power valve helps the output spread, particularly low down, but there is little real acceleration below 7,000rpm, whereupon it takes off explosively, peaking

out and fading by 9,500rpm. Keep it sweet in that 2,500rpm band through six close-ratio gears and the crisp acceleration and response is an exhilarating lesson in dynamics. The bike is unusually high geared especially in the lower ratios but the top speed of just over 140mph is not so significant as its fabulous, meaty acceleration. It is a real 'King of Quick' and a very well-finished engine. Held firmly in the narrow powerband, it behaves like a missile on a short fuse.

With so much free-flowing poke and sheer point-to-point rapidity, the rolling chassis needed to be something special and Yamaha's frame and suspension engineers have perfectly complemented and contained the excesses of the engine. Apart from the rear mono-shock being mounted longitudinally running under the motor, the chassis details are conventional but do a brilliant job. The LC steers quickly, it holds a line without wobbling or weaving, the ride is firm and well-damped and it has (and needs) three 10.5in brake discs that are tremendously powerful.

The arrival of the RD500LC marked a new era in motorcyling – the very same awesomely powerful two-stroke bikes that the factories were racing against each other in the GPs, were being suitably modified and released as road-going machines. Others quickly followed Yamaha's lead and the market is now full of street-legal, GP race weapons. Yamaha were first with a sleek, 392lb, 90bhp, V4 rocketship. It has been top of the pile ever since.

YAMAHA RD500LC	
Engine	liquid-cooled, 50 degree, V4, two-stroke
Cubic capacity	499cc
Maximum power	90bhp at 9500rpm
Bore × stroke	56.4 × 50mm
Gearbox	six-speed, constant mesh
Final drive	sealed, roller chain
Wheelbase	54.1in
Dry weight	392lb
Top speed	143mph
Standing quarter mile	11.8sec
Date of launch	1984

YAMAHA

RIGHT AND OPPOSITE BELOW RIGHT:
Small bike, big performance — the result of light weight and peaky power from Yamaha's race-developed 350cc two-stroke twin. The grand prix style power valve gives it good manners at low speeds, without compromising the giddy rush possible when revving hard and stirring up the six-speed gearbox.

YAMAHA RD350LC

THE RD350LC – the smallest-engined machine in our selection – earns a place because of its concept and design, as well as performance to the scale of a much bigger motorcycle. It is as near a racing lightweight as you can get without actually taking to the tracks.

Light, responsive, with excellent brakes, searing acceleration, and an eagerness for high revs, free use must be made of the slick six-speed gearbox to keep the Yamaha well on the boil. Properly ridden, it positively yowls along. What this means, on any road that is not arrow-straight, is that a skilful rider can outrun bikes that are far more powerful, and should by rights easily keep in front. Like a racer, the Yamaha looks for expertise in its rider, and rewards it hugely.

Other 'race-based' road bikes (including Yamaha's own RD500LC) can still claim the title fairly, though they have been substantially modified and detuned to make them more manageable and, inevitably, much slower than their original racing counterparts. Not so the LC350, based as it was on a smaller-engined class, with less than the outrageously difficult performance of the premier 500cc bikes.

Yamaha's racing 350s were the mainstay of the world championship class until it ended in 1982. The RD350LC brought the racing technology straight onto the road, with a twin-cradle 'featherbed' type of frame, monoshock suspension that was virtually copied from the racer, and a twin-cylinder engine that was more or less interchangeable.

Racing features of the first RD350-LC twin included water cooling to stabilize the temperatures which two-strokes find so critical. The next big step was the introduction of the Yamaha power valve system, an exhaust power valve that was itself a recent addition to the racers. This simple device varies exhaust port timing as the revs rise and fall, to improve the spread of power, and make the engine pull better at lower speeds. It makes the Yamaha easier to ride and easier to live with, without giving away any of the perky performance, and was retained on the next two models. One of these carried a race-style full fairing, to add a measure of weather protection as well as streamlining and a touch of style. The essential character remained that of a screaming two-stroke that turned a ride down the road into a passable imitation of a Grand Prix race.

The Yamaha's pure-bred sporting character attracts not only younger riders, who find its smaller engine size and lower all-up weight attractive, but also experienced motorcyclists who know how to get the best out of a machine that is not difficult to ride, but which still

offers a challenge to those who want to explore the limits of its performance. The bike is fast enough on the open road to break any speed limit, which makes it a realistic long-distance proposition. Certainly, the mono-shock rear suspension is comfortable for touring.

The best aspects of the bike come out on a mountain pass or through thick traffic when the surprising all-rounder comes into its agile, accelerative own. With the front wheel pawing the air in the lower gears and a faint haze of blue smoke, the RD350LC turns into a giant-killer again.

YAMAHA RD350LC YPVS	
Engine	liquid-cooled, two-stroke twin with YPVS
Cubic capacity	347cc
Maximum power	59bhp at 9000rpm
Bore × stroke	64 × 54mm
Gearbox	six-speed, constant mesh
Final drive	roller chain
Wheelbase	54.5in
Dry weight	364lb
Top speed	121mph
Standing quarter mile	13sec
Date of launch	1983

YAMAHA

JAPAN

RIGHT AND INSET: *Frame tubes painted bright silver emphasized the point that the Yamaha FJ1100 has the first of a new generation of frames ... the tubes come around the side of the engine, instead of over the top. Other tricks to make a powerful heavyweight handle more like a middleweight included small 16in wheels back and front.*

YAMAHA FJ1100

THE FJ1100 was the first litre-plus motorcycle to address the problem of all litre-plus motorcycles – how to make something fundamentally big and heavy handle responsively. The FJ is a genuine 150mph superbike, combining a huge and immensely strong engine with a low and fairly lightweight chassis. Until the FJ1200, it was Yamaha's flagship, their biggest and most powerful four-stroke motorcycle.

The motor is a compact, slightly inclined, DOHC, 16 valve transverse four, remarkable only for the amount of sheer, outright power it gives – 125bhp at 9,000rpm – which makes the FJ a king of wheelspin along its rapid path to a blistering top speed. What is unusual about the bike is the way the engine is mounted. Yamaha realized that serious weight-saving on a bike this big was a futile exercise, so they concentrated their efforts on keeping the weight, and indeed the bike, low and compact. Their 'lateral frame concept' consists of a high-tensile, box-section steel frame built along endurance racer lines. There are no top tubes running above the engine. Instead, two huge frame tubes laterally hug the motor's sides. Instead of meeting at the steering head, these two side tubes join in front of it; the steering pivot itself is supported by small-diameter tubing, fully triangulated off these main rails. The aim is to achieve the greatest possible steering head rigidity. Certainly it was a first for a Japanese production bike.

Sitting on 16in wheels, front and back, the FJ1100 feels remarkably low on the road. The seat height is a mere 30.7in yet there is good ground clearance. With a full tank it weighs 556lb yet the weight is hardly noticeable on the move. The bike's low and tight dimensions belie its size and it has none of the dead, top heavy feel of traditional 1100cc monster road bikes. It steers quickly and nimbly as intended. On small wheels with fat tyres, 4.4in of trail, a 30 degree head angle and a trim 58.3in wheelbase, the FJ was the first 1100 to prove as lively as many a middleweight motorcycle.

It makes smooth and strong power effortlessly. The wind-tunnel designed full fairing deflects the worst of the wind and the weather and helps the bike to an impressive top speed. It is so quick and powerful that it can easily deceive the rider about what speed he or she is doing.

Early in 1986, Yamaha unveiled the FJ1200, an oversized big bore version with more power everywhere especially in the midrange. It is only a few mph faster at the top end. The chassis spec is virtually identical and only detail changes have been made. The 1200 is the new flagship of Yamaha's four-stroke fleet and the biggest capacity sports tourer in the world.

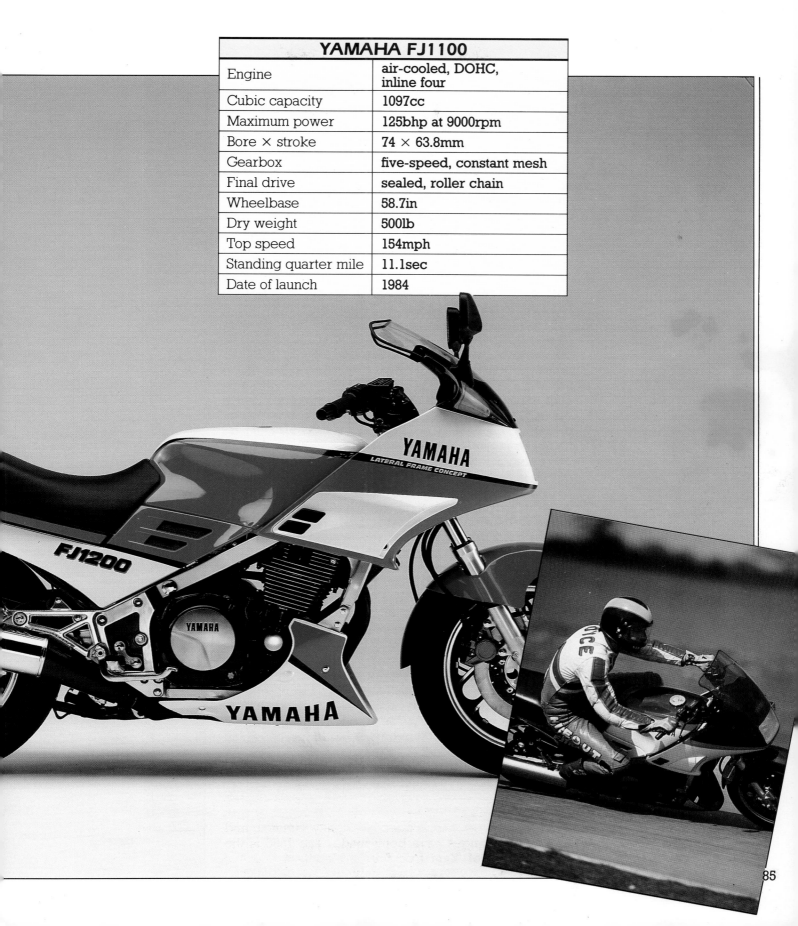

YAMAHA FJ1100

Engine	air-cooled, DOHC, inline four
Cubic capacity	1097cc
Maximum power	125bhp at 9000rpm
Bore × stroke	74 × 63.8mm
Gearbox	five-speed, constant mesh
Final drive	sealed, roller chain
Wheelbase	58.7in
Dry weight	500lb
Top speed	154mph
Standing quarter mile	11.1sec
Date of launch	1984

YAMAHA

JAPAN

RIGHT AND OPPOSITE BELOW RIGHT:
It goes even better when
you take the front brake off
... the 20-valve
four-cylinder Yamaha is a
leader of the new breed of
superquick 750s that follow
a racing formula to
challenge the heavier full
1,000cc heavyweights.

YAMAHA FZ750

THIS motorcycle is a pure sports sensation, firmly in the vanguard of modern performance dynamics. Yamaha describe the FZ as 'a total performance motorcycle', and it would be hard to disagree with them. The FZ750 has one of the most sophisticated engines around. It gives as much speed and horsepower as most 1100cc bikes but its electrifying performance is more usable because it handles well too. Everything about the FZ750 is state of the art, yet it does not have a radical, sports only, riding position nor was it bred directly from the race track. Yamaha designers created it from scratch as a potent, versatile all-rounder. The result is one of the very best road bikes currently available.

At the heart of the FZ is one of the most powerful and free-revving engines of all time. Each of the four cylinders uses five valves – three inlet, two exhaust. Yamaha had experimented with six and seven valves per cylinder but five proved best for all-round power and efficiency.

In pursuit of power, the shape of the combustion chamber was redesigned and the FZ runs a big 11.2:1 compression ratio. The most visually striking feature of the engine is the forwardly inclined cylinders. The advantages of leaning an inline four forward by 45 degrees are numerous. It allows Yamaha to use downdraft carburettors giving a straighter induction path and better cylinder filling. More importantly the inclined engine has a very positive effect on handling, stability, braking and even riding position.

The engine performance is phenomenal, giving smooth power all the way from 3,000rpm to well beyond the 11,000rpm redline. It revs so freely and so hard that Yamaha had to fit a rev limiter to stop it exceeding 12,000rpm and possibly tangling its 20 lightweight valves. The power curve is almost perfect, wide with a flat, hard-pulling torque curve, consistently higher anywhere along the rev range than any other 750. Acceleration is out of this world. The mid-range power will spin the rear tyre and forceful pick-up is on tap anywhere between 4,000 and 7,000rpm. Top end performance is unparalleled, from 100 to 145mph is but a flick of the wrist. In top gear roll-on tests, it will destroy anything but a turbo, particularly low down because of its low gearing. It is a bike for all speeds and all seasons designed to take on all-comers. By tilting the engine forward in the frame, the centre of gravity was lowered and weight put usefully on the front wheel. Since the carburettors are tucked in close behind the steering head, Yamaha were able to use a large gas tank cleverly designed to carry the consider-

able fuel weight low down behind the engine instead of above it. Fuel is fed to the carburettors by an electric pump. All this makes for sharp handling and allows the quick-steering advantage of a steep head angle to be combined with a short wheelbase. The FZ is stable and flickable, with excellent brakes and ground clearance.

Yamaha have long dominated the two-stroke scene and many observers thought that they were incapable of building a competitive, truly sporting four-stroke. The FZ, planned and created in secret, gave that view the lie when it was finally uncaged.

It is the narrowest inline four cylinder machine ever built, and one of the most powerful. It is under-stated yet technologically advanced. For Yamaha the FZ was a giant step towards 'total performance'. The bike took the market and other manufacturers by surprise and has set standards of 750cc performance that will be difficult to equal, let alone surpass.

YAMAHA FZ750	
Engine	liquid-cooled, DOHC, inline four
Cubic capacity	749cc
Maximum power	100bhp at 10,500rpm
Bore × stroke	68 × 51.6mm
Gearbox	six-speed, constant mesh
Final drive	sealed, roller chain
Wheelbase	58.5in
Dry weight	460lb
Top speed	146mph
Standing quarter mile	10.8sec
Date of launch	1985

YAMAHA

JAPAN

RIGHT: *Yamaha's V-Max is closely related to movie maniac Mad Max, if only in spirit. Its prime purpose is to cover the quarter-mile in the quickest possible time. To that end, a massively powerful V4 engine crowds the engine bay. Chrome air-scoops are real — what looks like a fuel tank is in reality an air-filter housing. The gas is carried under the rider's seat.*

YAMAHA V-MAX

AMAHA's V-Max is designed to excel in the acceleration field. Its top speed of around 135mph is not as high as it might be, given a monstrous V4 engine with a power output of 135bhp, and compared with race-replica models. What is sensational is how quickly it gets to that speed. Acceleration is the V-Max's reason for being, helped by the fat rear tyre like that of a drag bike and gearing to match.

Launched in 1984, the V-Max became at once the ultimate hot rod, the fastest-accelerating road bike ever, sizzling through the standing quarter mile in not quite ten seconds. Ten years before, only specialized dragsters could accelerate like that.

The basis of this factory hot rod was the big V4 engine from Yamaha's Venture tourer – a veritable river-barge of a bike, festooned with fairings and luggage gear. All that went, and the V-Max was left behind, spare but still monstrous, its styling dominated by the massive engine with two giant air-scoops for the four down-draught carburettors where you would expect to see the fuel tank. The V-Max, like the Venture, has a low-slung tank beneath the seat, with the fuel pumped up to the four greedy carburettor throats.

A vestigial pillion seat completed the spartan look, while the back tyre behind it was of unprecedented width: a 150/90 × 15 monster.

The engine was revitalized to release more of its fire-breathing potential, with the output rising from 90bhp in Venture trim to a massive 135bhp as the V-Max. The factory hop-up job was thorough, including a stronger crankshaft, lightened pistons with a 10.5:1 compression ratio, bigger valves, and high-lift double overhead camshafts. Yamaha also introduced a novel system of automatic butterfly valves linking the inlet tracts below the carburettors, which smoothed out the power delivery right across the rev range. The V-Max retained the shaft drive of the touring bike, freeing the owner from the burden of replacing shattered rear chains and the hard-worked rear tyre.

In a straight line, there is nothing to touch the V-Max. The way it hunkers down and takes off leaves all its rivals gasping. If its handling on a twisty road is a bit twitchy, it makes up so much ground *between* the bends that it hardly matters.

On a long high-speed run, the rider – sitting upright and holding onto high and wide handlebars – feels like a parachute as the wind catches the chest. This more or less confined the V-Max's usefulness to the USA, where low speed limits favour fast acceleration at the expense of top speed. Europe did not see the V-Max, except as a spectre of the imagination.

YAMAHA V-MAX

Engine	liquid-cooled, 72 degree, V4 with V-Boost
Cubic capacity	1198cc
Maximum power	143bhp at 8500rpm
Bore × stroke	76 × 66mm
Gearbox	five-speed, constant mesh
Final drive	shaft
Wheelbase	62.6in
Dry weight	596lb
Top speed	141mph
Standing quarter mile	10.3sec
Date of launch	1984

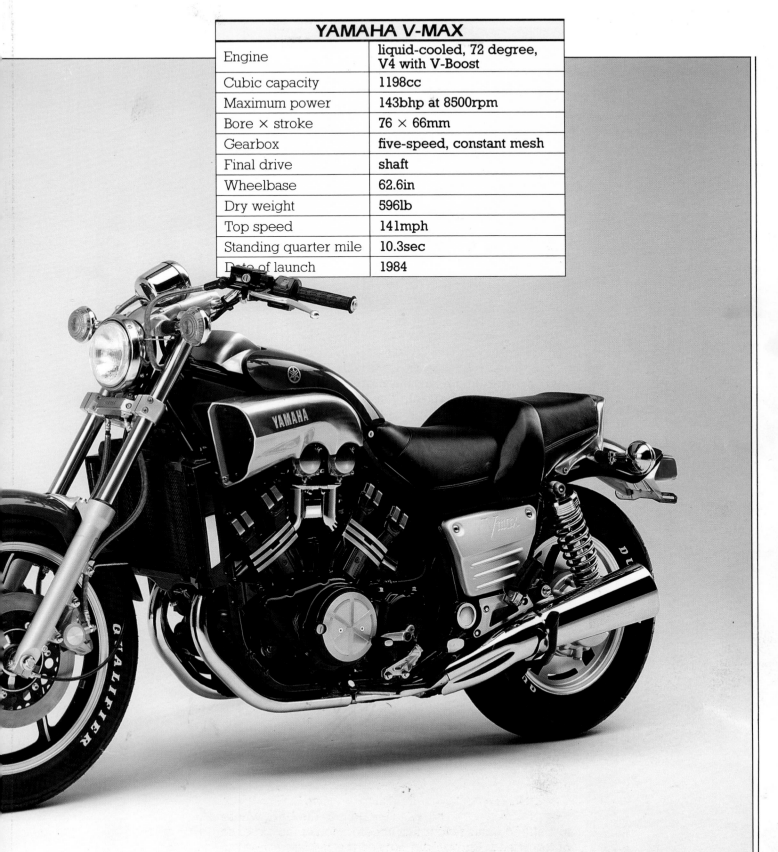

PREVIOUS PAGE: *British star Rob McElnea on the Heron-Suzuki RG500 — creative British chassis design and a Japanese engine.*

RIGHT AND OPPOSITE BELOW RIGHT: *Sensationally different, the Elf 2 seeks new solutions to age old problems. If it works at racing speeds it will be more than good enough for the road.*

ELF 2

OICHIRO 'Pops' Honda himself is on record as saying that in 20 years time, all motorcycles will look like the Elf. Certainly this machine wears the face of the future.

The Elf is a radical departure from two-wheel tradition, but the technology behind it is familiar, drawn mainly from the world of racing cars. This is hardly surprising as the designer Andre de Cortanze previously worked with the Renault Formula One car team.

The Elf concept first appeared on the race-tracks in the late 1970s as an endurance racer powered by a four-cylinder Honda engine. Though it performed creditably, this early prototype version never finished a race. However, it made a big impression, particularly with its stability under hard braking compared with conventional bikes.

The Grand Prix racing version first appeared during 1984 and was raced in 1985. Again the bike failed to come up with the results. This was hardly surprising considering as it was a brand-new design competing against machines that have been developed for generations.

The guiding design principles of the Elf are lightness, keeping the weight low and rigidity, combined with a front suspension to improve on the flawed design of telescopic front forks. At the heart of the machine is a Honda NS500 V3 two-stroke engine. More than just the heart – the engine casings, reinforced by aluminium plates, are the frame, providing pick-up points for the front and rear suspension.

At the front, the Elf is like a car's double wishbone system turned through 90 degrees, with the two arms running round the right of the wheel to locate the steering king-pin in the centre (special, deeply-dished wheels had to be made). The suspension arms themselves were made of cast magnesium, though the top one was sometimes replaced by a tubular structure that allowed modifications to be made more easily.

At the rear of the bike, a single trailing arm of massive section operates a rising-rate linkage for the single damper. Unusually, the drive sprocket is on the opposite side of the arm from the wheel, so the arm actually passes between the chain runs.

Various suspension experiments have been seen. At first, both front and rear springs and dampers were horizontally mounted beneath the engine. Later they were moved to opposite diagonal corners of the engine. Occasionally they were linked by a torsion bar to provide anti-pitch in the same way as a roll bar links the front wheels of a car.

The fuel is carried beneath the engine with the

exhausts running over the top of it, and a single body-work moulding provides a cover, a seat, and streamlining.

By the end of 1985, the Elf 2 had made little impression on the GP results with a string of non-finishes. Teething problems included unexpected wheel hop under braking (where the endurance bike had been much better). This was only to be expected, perhaps, when venturing into unknown territory. Certainly the lack-lustre start has not discouraged the Honda factory from supporting the project. With help like that, the Elf seems assured of a fast-forward path into the future.

ELF 2	
Engine	liquid-cooled, 90 degree, V3 two-stroke
Cubic capacity	499cc
Maximum power	more than 130bhp
Bore × stroke	62.6 × 54mm
Gearbox	six-speed, constant mesh
Final drive	chain
Wheelbase	54.5in
Dry weight	approx. 270lb
Top speed	more than 165mph
Date of launch	1984

Freddie Spencer on the NSR500 Honda — an almost unbeatable combination. Note the low level exhausts of the MkII version of the bike.

HONDA NSR500

ONDA's answer to Yamaha's V4 was another V4 – the NSR500. But the world's largest motorcycle factory wanted to beat Yamaha, not just copy them. The result is a very different motorcycle.

The NSR500 is usually faster than the Yamaha, and it has the great asset of starting up quicker, firing on all four cylinders after the pushing rider has taken only a couple of steps. But racing is swings and roundabouts, with the pace of engine development meaning that rivals tend to leapfrog ahead of one another with each new engineering trick.

Honda released the NSR in 1984, exclusively for reigning champion Freddie Spencer. The first version was unorthodox in layout with the fuel carried beneath the engine and the four exhaust expansion chambers running over the top. What looked like a normal fuel tank was in fact a heat shield. This design kept the weight low down but this made access to the engine rather difficult – especially at critical moments.

The design for 1985 was revised with the fuel tank back on top and the exhausts beneath . . . and Spencer regained the 500cc world title from Yamaha and Eddie Lawson.

There is a great deal of secrecy concerning the engine details. Some things are, however, visible to the onlooker. The Honda is a true V4, all cylinders on a single crankshaft, with an angle of 90 degrees between the vee. Especially narrow low-friction bearings have prevented the engine from acquiring excessive width, but it is still wider than any two-crankshaft design.

A set of four carburettors within the vee feed the cylinders via crank-case reed valves. There is a multiplate dry clutch, a six-speed gearbox and chain final drive. Honda's version of the exhaust power valve, ATAC, operates on all four cylinders controlled by a centrifugal governor.

It is also possible to discern – when a mechanic blips the throttle – that the engine is exceptionally responsive because of minimized internal friction and that it is almost free from vibration.

When Spencer rides the NSR500 its other attributes become obvious. It is powerful enough to induce harmonic vibrations in tyre, suspension and frame, and also to accelerate at a visibly faster rate than any other machine on the track.

The frame of this hand-built motorcycle (only seven examples have been made, and four ever seen together) is fairly conventional: a twin-spar design made from rectangular-section aluminium tubing, with a pivoted rear fork operating a rising-rate linkage to the single Showa damper. The front forks echo Honda's

road-bike practice (or vice versa), with a similar principal of hydraulic anti-dive linked to movement of the brake calipers.

What separates the bike from its roadgoing stablemates is its rarity and the sort of attention that sees as many as six technicians flocking around it every time it pulls up – a tyre man, a rear suspension man, a front suspension man, a brake man . . . Despite the expense involved in its manufacture and the care in its maintenance, the NSR500 will last for less than a year before it is discarded, to be put in a museum, or destroyed.

HONDA NSR500	
Engine	liquid-cooled, 90 degree, V4 two-stroke
Cubic capacity	495cc
Maximum power	more than 140bhp
Bore × stroke	54 × 54mm
Gearbox	six-speed, constant mesh
Final drive	chain
Wheelbase	54.1in
Dry weight	283lb
Top speed	more than 175mph
Date of launch	1984

RIGHT AND OPPOSITE ABOVE RIGHT: *The definitive endurance racer, Honda's RVF750 is based on a road bike, with no expense spared in preparing it for the 24-hour tracks. Note the single rear trailing arm suspension — allowing for very quick wheel changes mid-race.*

HONDA RVF750

THIS bike is currently the most successful four-stroke racer in the world. Since both the Endurance and Formula One World Championships adopted a capacity ceiling of 750cc in 1984, the RVF has won both titles in consecutive years. In the gruelling world of endurance racing, the bike has proved virtually unbeatable. It is a complete, proven and above all consistent and reliable machine, perfectly capable of being run flat out for 24 hours, day and night, and needing only a regular diet of petrol, oil, tyres, brake pads . . . and riders.

Endurance, F-One and Superbike racing are the last bastion for big four-strokes and the machines are of much more relevance to the road user than the high-tech weaponry of the Grand Prix, since the engines must be based on available road bikes. It is a competitive affair and Suzuki's GSX-R and Yamaha's FZ have proved to be strong contenders for the Honda's crown. To date, however, they have come nowhere near matching the Honda V4's overwhelming, overall dominance.

The RVF is based on Honda's VF and VFR750. They both have a water-cooled, 90 degree, V4 engine with gear driven DOHC, four-valve heads and a 748cc capacity. Almost everything else is completely different and exclusive to the factory racer. The endurance bike makes a maximum of 130bhp at 12,000rpm. It uses a rev limiter designed to cut in at 12,500rpm during the six and eight hour races though this is dropped to 12,000rpm for the 24 hour marathons. With a five speed gearbox and a choice of three possible primary drive ratios, the Honda is geared for a top speed in excess of 170mph. More importantly, the engine produces its power very smoothly with a wide spread of torque. This makes it very tractable, an obvious bonus if the rider has to face typically varied endurance racing weather – sunshine during the day, rain at night and freezing fog at dawn.

The frame, in box-section aluminium, with the engine stressed is very similar to the twin spar frames used by Honda on their 250 and 500cc two-stroke GP racers. Suspension is by Showa all round and at the back there is a very interesting one-sided, aluminium swing-arm with an inboard disc and dished wheel. This makes for very quick wheel changes, an essential part of all long distance racing. The 18in rear wheel, wearing a Michelin radial slick, can be changed in under 10 seconds flat.

The brakes are fully floating with four piston, Nissan calipers. The dry weight of the bike is 350lb. Since its debut as the official factory racer run under the Honda France banner, the RVF has beaten all-comers and

proved immensely reliable. A competitive endurance bike needs not only speed but also strength. The RVF rarely breaks down. In the expert hands of the reigning World Champions, Gerard Coudray and Patrick Igoa, it has been crashed only a handful of times in two years and has invariably been patched up quickly and efficiently enough to rejoin the fray.

Endurance racing is an expensive, time consuming and gloriously imaginative affair, an exacting test of both men and machines, passionately supported in Europe and Japan. The equation for success is full of imponderables. Riders need to be hard yet adaptable with a disciplined and well-organized pit support crew. Above all a very reliable and plain, quick motorcycle is necessary. The RVF is currently the best there is and shows no sign of relaxing its stranglehold on the World Endurance title. The bike has emerged over thousands of miles against the 'stop', in all weathers, as the leading contender for major honours. An endurance racer supreme.

HONDA RVF750	
Engine	liquid-cooled, DOHC, 90 degree, V4
Cubic capacity	748cc
Maximum power	130bhp at 12000rpm
Bore × stroke	70 × 40.8mm
Gearbox	five-speed, constant mesh
Final drive	chain
Wheelbase	55.2in
Dry weight	350lb
Top speed	more than 170mph
Date of launch	1985

⚡ SUZUKI

Two versions of Suzuki's RG500.
RIGHT: *World Champion Franco Uncini's bike uses an aluminium frame.*
INSET: *The British team developed a revolutionary light-weight chassis using carbon fibre-honeycomb nicknamed 'Cardboard Box'.*

SUZUKI RG500

THE Suzuki RG500 is the longest-lived racing design of the 1980s (and is shortly to be superceded). This bike took part in the dawn of two-stroke domination to the top 500cc class of road racing and wrote its name large in the record books.

The square-four Suzuki took Barry Sheene to the first of two world championships in 1976. Altogether four riders' titles have been won on this Suzuki, and the bikes took the manufacturers' championship for seven consecutive years.

The RG500 has been through several evolutionary changes since its introduction. The engine has been made more compact by 'stepping' the pairs of cylinders, while increased power has been sought by introducing a type of exhaust chamber similar in concept to Honda's. The most significant development towards the end of the RG500's long racing life came not from Japan but Britain, where the local importers introduced a radical new frame design and construction that promises to take Suzuki's new engine to a future perhaps as significant as the old engine's past.

The Heron-Suzuki broke new ground in motorcycling by dispensing with the traditional tubular or fabricated sheet steel or aluminium frame. Instead, they introduced a material already widely used both in aircraft and in racing cars – a honeycomb sandwich-board made in England by Ciba-Geigy.

The Heron-Suzuki team, with designer Nigel Leaper, constructed what was basically a box around the engine, earning the 1984 bike the nickname 'Cardboard Box'. The steering head was located by a triangular section in the top front corner, with aluminium inserts locating the fork pivot at the rear.

The RG500 was an immediate success with rider Rob McElnea. However, a lack of power compared with the more recently designed Yamaha and Honda V4 engines kept the bike out of the top results.

For 1985, though still lacking a really competitive engine, the team developed the concept further. Carbon-fibre was used in place of aluminium which saved more weight and gave added strength. By the end of the season even the rear aluminium swing-arm had been replaced by a composite-material item.

1986 was expected to be the last season for the doughty RG500, the bike that had spawned imitators from Yamaha, and fathered a line of production racers and eventually even a road bike. Suzuki were expected to produce a new V4 engine, to take up the challenge yet again.

Only one thing would remain from the old bike ... the British frame.

SUZUKI RG500	
Engine	liquid-cooled, square-four, two-stroke
Cubic capacity	498cc
Maximum power	125bhp
Bore × stroke	56 × 50.6mm
Gearbox	six-speed, constant mesh
Final drive	chain
Wheelbase	55.2in
Dry weight	250lb
Top speed	more than 170mph
Year of launch	1975

YAMAHA

JAPAN

Steady development has made Yamaha's V4 YZR into the definitive 500cc grand prix racer. Note the hand-made aluminium frame.
RIGHT: *Here, team-mates Raymond Roche and world champion Eddie Lawson* (OPPOSITE ABOVE RIGHT) *put it to the test.*

YAMAHA YZR500

GRAND prix racing motorcycle is designed for only one purpose . . . to get past the chequered flag first after some 75 miles of racing. To do this, it needs to be very fast, but that is not all. It must also have good brakes, agile roadholding and be reliable. It is this combination which produces a winner.

Yamaha's YZR500 is an exemplary racing motorcycle. Winner of the world championship for rider Eddie Lawson in 1984, the bike is not only fast but is reliable enough to have completed more than three consecutive seasons on the run without a single breakdown. With the high-stress engineering inseparable from ultimate performance, that is an achievement indeed.

YZR500 is a generic name covering several generations of Yamaha racers. The YZR in question is the latest version, the V4, that began life as the OW61 of 1982 and by 1985 had become the OW81. Although the latest bike is much changed in detail, the fundamental design has remained the same.

The engine is not a true V4. Two separate pairs of oversquare cylinders are arranged in a vee, but each has its own crankshaft which is geared together to drive the multiplate dry clutch. Perhaps it should be called a W4. In this, it follows Yamaha's long-established racing pattern, and can trace its ancestry back to the YZR500 inline four, which also had two crankshafts, placed end to end, and the following square four, with the pairs of cylinders one behind the other. They were rearranged in a vee (or W) in 1983, for Kenny Roberts' last grand prix year.

In this form, the engine used disc valves to control induction, cleverly arranged and bevel-driven within the vee between the cylinders. Turning at half engine speed, each valve served two cylinders. However, in 1984, Yamaha followed Honda's lead in introducing reed-valve induction, primarily to make the bike start quicker in the dead-engine grand prix push-starts.

A six-speed gearbox is behind the engine, and final drive is by chain just like a road bike.

The Yamaha frame is an exercise in robust lightweight construction. Fabricated from sheet aluminium it takes the form of a twin-spar structure. Front suspension is by telescopic forks with multi-adjustable damping. The anti-dive mechanism was removed in 1985 as it offered no positive benefits on a race-track. The rear pivoted fork (or swing-arm) is also strongly constructed from lightweight aluminium, and operates a rising-rate linkage to compress the single Ohlins damper.

Power has risen through the years until it is now more than 140 horsepower – enough to give the bike blinding

acceleration and a top speed in the region of 180mph. Even with sticky 'slick' tyres, keeping such a machine from either flipping over backwards or sliding off the road demands experience. Riding the bike to its limits requires exceptional skill. The rewards for developing such a skill could be a world championship.

YAMAHA YZR500 OW81	
Engine	liquid-cooled, 60 degree, W4 two-stroke
Cubic capacity	498cc
Maximum power	approx. 140bhp
Bore × stroke	56 × 50.6mm
Gearbox	six-speed, constant mesh
Final drive	chain
Wheelbase	54.4in
Dry weight	288lb
Top speed	more than 175mph
Date of launch	1982

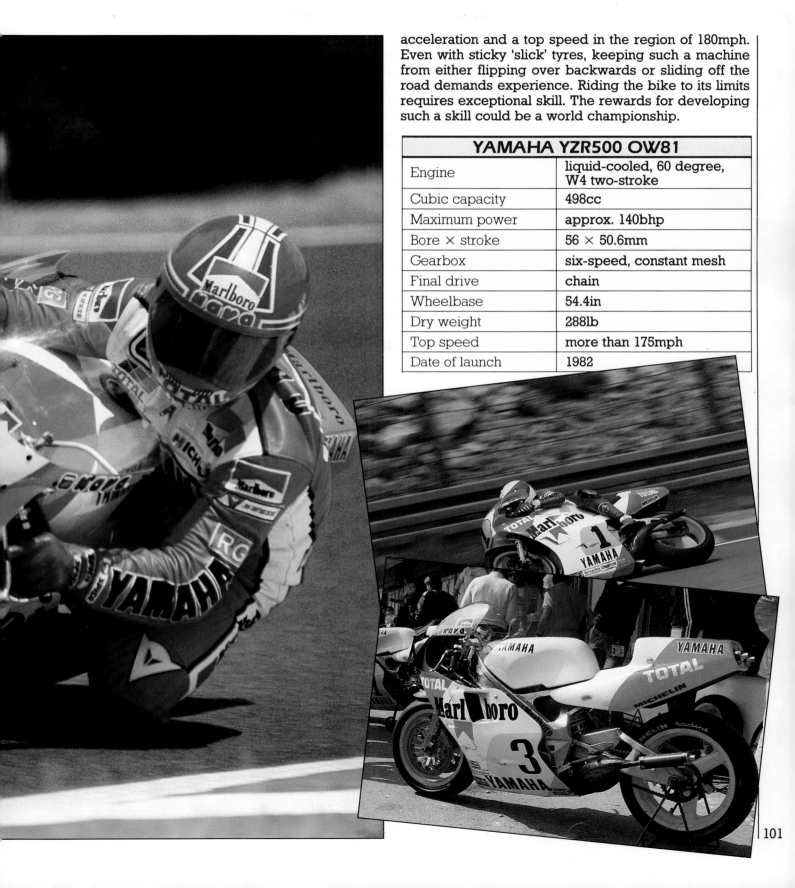

SUPERBIKING POWERHOUSE

T was once the aim of the racing engine designer to achieve 100 horsepower for every litre of capacity. He was prepared to make all kinds of sacrifices to achieve this – an engine that would not idle, that was hard to start, and that used as much fuel as it liked. Power was the main consideration.

Modern motorcycle engines have made a nonsense of those figures. It is a poor machine that does not better 100bhp/litre. The achievement today is to make the engine that is quiet, clean and as polite as a country cleric's runabout, yet capable of revving like a race bike, and of doing it almost indefinitely.

The modern superbike would have reached its current stage of development without the computer, but it would have taken much longer. Computer design techniques offer not only the facility for rapid and comprehensive calculation, but also the chance to perform simulations of both frame and engine design variations without cutting or casting any metal. In the end there is no substitute for bench- or road-testing, but today many variations can be tried and many corners cut on the way.

In the engine

Four new techniques in motorcycle engines both deliver the goods now, and promise more improvement in the future.

The first is the oil-cooling system developed by Suzuki for their GSX-R750 and 1100 models; the second is the electronic engine management equipment used by BMW and Kawasaki for their top models; the third is the swirl-promoting combustion chambers common to many engines; and the fourth applies only to two-strokes – the variable exhaust geometry that has radically improved the spread of power without impairing the ultimate quantity at high revs.

The prime benefit of Suzuki's oil cooling is in reduction of engine weight. The four-cylinder units carry the same amount of metal as a conventional finned and air-cooled machine, yet offer the close temperature control of liquid-cooled engines *without* carrying all the extra weight of water-jackets, pipes and radiators, not to mention the coolant itself.

It can be argued that all engines are oil-cooled. Circulation of the lubricant, especially over the cylinder heads, inevitably removes heat from the hot spots, and redistributes it to colder parts of the engine. Suzuki's trick (and it is not a new technique, originally dating back to the 1930s) is to reinforce this property by deliberate design. Their engine not only carries extra oil, but also a second oil-circulating system, supplementing the high-pressure lubrication, and devoted purely to washing oil over the hot spots in liberal quantities.

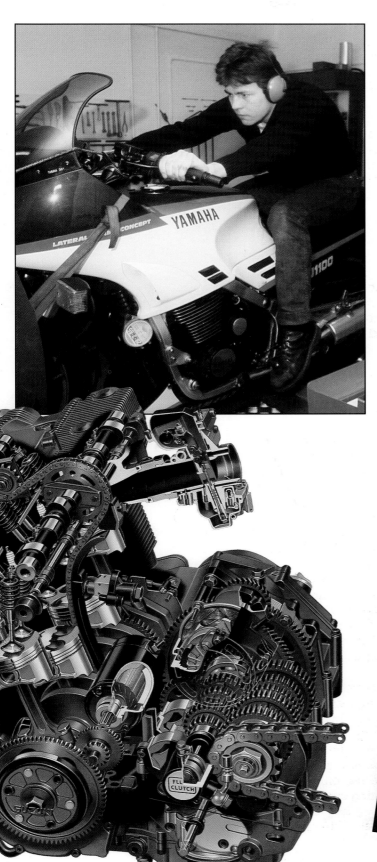

Remove the camshaft covers and it is plain to see how a cascade of oil is directed over the cylinder heads, especially in the area of the exhaust ports, the hottest part of the engine. The oil runs back to the sump by gravity and then is pumped through a radiator to shed its heat.

Good cooling allows an engine with closer tolerances. It improves longevity and full-throttle stamina and allows for higher tuning with less risk. Suzuki have achieved all these benefits without the weight and complication of a separate external cooling system, and it paid instant dividends on road and race-track.

Electronic engine management was introduced in a limited form by Kawasaki and brought to the next level by BMW. Two areas are affected, ignition and fuel supply, and the more sophisticated system integrates the two so that just one 'brain' does it all.

Computer-controlled electronic ignition is nothing new. Electronic sensors take the place of mechanical contact-breaker points to measure crankshaft rotation, and specifically the point where the sparking plug is triggered to fire (some time before the piston reaches top dead centre, to allow for combustion delays). Simultaneously, the 'brain' is informed of what speed the engine is turning, and the amount of throttle opening (via the inlet manifold vacuum). Pre-programmed cir-

cuits then impose secondary instructions that override the trigger, to advance the timing as revs rise, or to retard it to make the engine easier to start, with all sorts of shades in between.

The timing of the spark is not only exact, but can be tailored to the characteristics of an individual engine design. The system is also amenable to the introduction of a rev-limiter, which kills the sparks to avoid engine damage after a missed gearchange, for example.

Computerized control of the fuel mixture is more complex, and is a process in which carburettors can play no part. It is essential to have electronic fuel injection.

RIGHT: *BMW's K-series models introduced integrated electronic engine management, with computers controlling ignition and fuel injection.* OPPOSITE ABOVE LEFT: *The fuel injection replaces carburettors with compact and simple-looking tubes and even the speedometer, rev counter and digital clock (*OPPOSITE ABOVE RIGHT*) are electronically operated.*

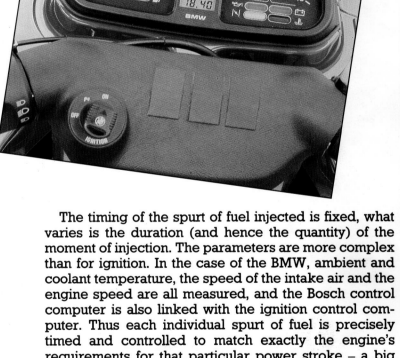

The timing of the spurt of fuel injected is fixed, what varies is the duration (and hence the quantity) of the moment of injection. The parameters are more complex than for ignition. In the case of the BMW, ambient and coolant temperature, the speed of the intake air and the engine speed are all measured, and the Bosch control computer is also linked with the ignition control computer. Thus each individual spurt of fuel is precisely timed and controlled to match exactly the engine's requirements for that particular power stroke – a big advance over the hit-or-miss nature of a carburettor.

The benefits are immediately obvious – easy starting and better fuel economy. The cleaner exhaust gases are harder to measure. Electronic engine management is likely to become more common in the near future.

Not so turbo-charging, which enjoyed a brief vogue, but never achieved the popularity on two wheels that it has on four. The main reason for this is inherent in the nature of the system.

Turbo-charging uses the energy of gases escaping down the exhaust pipe to spin a turbine, which is in turn connected to another turbine which pressurizes the intake system, packing in more fuel/air mixture in the same way as the classic supercharger.

ABOVE: *The goal is super-speed, and privately modified bikes like this 1100cc Kawasaki and 1138cc Suzuki (ABOVE RIGHT) each have turbochargers and nitrous-oxide injection ... note the laughing gas bottles strapped on the rear.*

OPPOSITE ABOVE LEFT: *For two-strokes, Yamaha's rotary exhaust power valve system allows high tuning without bad manners.*

OPPOSITE ABOVE RIGHT: *A factory turbo installation is neat and effective — this is a Kawasaki 750 Turbo.*

If the exhaust pressure is low, with the engine at low revs or small throttle openings, the turbo-charger consequently turns very slowly or not at all. It needs the engine to be driving hard before it can reach working speed (in excess of 20,000rpm), and make it drive harder still.

Motorcycles use relatively small engines, exhaling small amounts of gas. Most existing turbo-chargers were simply too large to work at anything except the very highest revs. Thus fitment to a motorcycle engine imposed sluggish response and a delay in answering the throttle in the engine's most common working rev range – the dreaded turbo lag. They only started to yield benefits when the motorcycle was already going fast.

Even so, all four Japanese manufacturers offered turbo-charged models. Honda's in particular was a masterpiece of complexity, attempting to overcome the turbo's disadvantages with a full house of electronic engine controls. However, the CX500 Turbo performed little better than a normally aspirated 750 model, was heavier, more expensive, and the throttle response was worse. Motorcycles do not need turbo-chargers. If you are short of power buy a model with a bigger engine.

There is another system that gives a spurt of extra power on demand, with no delays. It is nitrous oxide injection ... laughing gas. Simply, a pressure bottle of gas is fitted to the motorcycle and plumbed into the intake system. Press a button on the handlebars and the

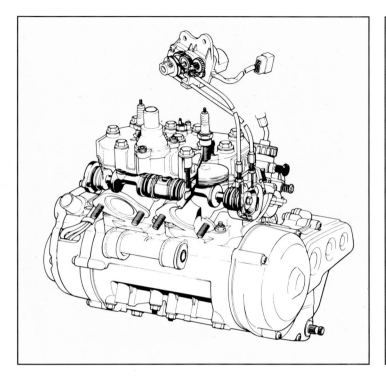

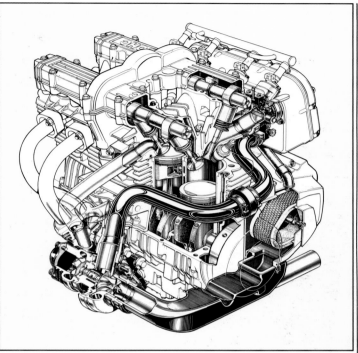

gas enters the combustion chamber where it breaks down in the combustion process to release oxygen. The only other component that is necessary is an extra spurt of petrol to go in with it, and it has the same effect as instant supercharging.

No production bike has ever been fitted with nitrous oxide injection, but it can be bought as an accessory. Simple to install, devastating in its results, the only drawback is the short-term effect ... and that you quickly use up the amount of gas that it is convenient to carry. For guaranteed results, adding as much as 50 per cent to your power output in a split second, there is nothing quite like laughing gas.

The factories rely on more subtle effects to improve performance. The third item in our quartet of stars of modern engineering is improved combustion by swirl induction. This means that the fuel/air mixture enters the combustion chamber in a turbulent state, so many eddies and whirlpools. When the sparking plug sets it on fire, the turbulence spreads the flame front quickly through the entire chamber. Combustion is faster, more complete, and more efficient – leading to more power and better economy.

There are several different ways of doing this, many with acronymic titles. YICS (Yamaha intake controlled swirl) is a system that links intake ports with angled high-velocity tubes, while Suzuki's TSCC (twin swirl combustion chamber) is a four-valve system that feeds a pair of linked chambers within each head.

The most technically complex is Yamaha's latest cylinder head, with an unprecedented *five* valves. Two serve the exhaust, another two the inlet. The fifth is an ancillary inlet valve shooting an extra jet of mixture in at an angle to the main flow.

Finally – two-strokes. Here recent advances have concentrated on the exhaust geometry. The back-pressure of the exhaust is vital to improve the compression of the engine, since the port remains open after the cylinder has filled with mixture and has begun compression. Modern tuning techniques use the harmonics of the exhaust's resonance to send pressure waves back to 'close' the port before the piston has done so. The problem is that the harmonics remain constant but the revs rise and fall, so the harmonic that suits full power at high revs may be quite wrong over the rest of

BELOW: *This liquid-cooled Kawasaki off-road bike has long-travel leading-axle front forks, and a rising-rate linkage operating the single rear spring.*
CENTRE: *Kawasaki's GPz1000 road bike has more compact rear suspension, and a 'perimeter frame' that runs around the sides of the engine.*
OPPOSITE ABOVE RIGHT: *Honda's V3 NS400 engine showing the ATAC exhaust power chambers.*

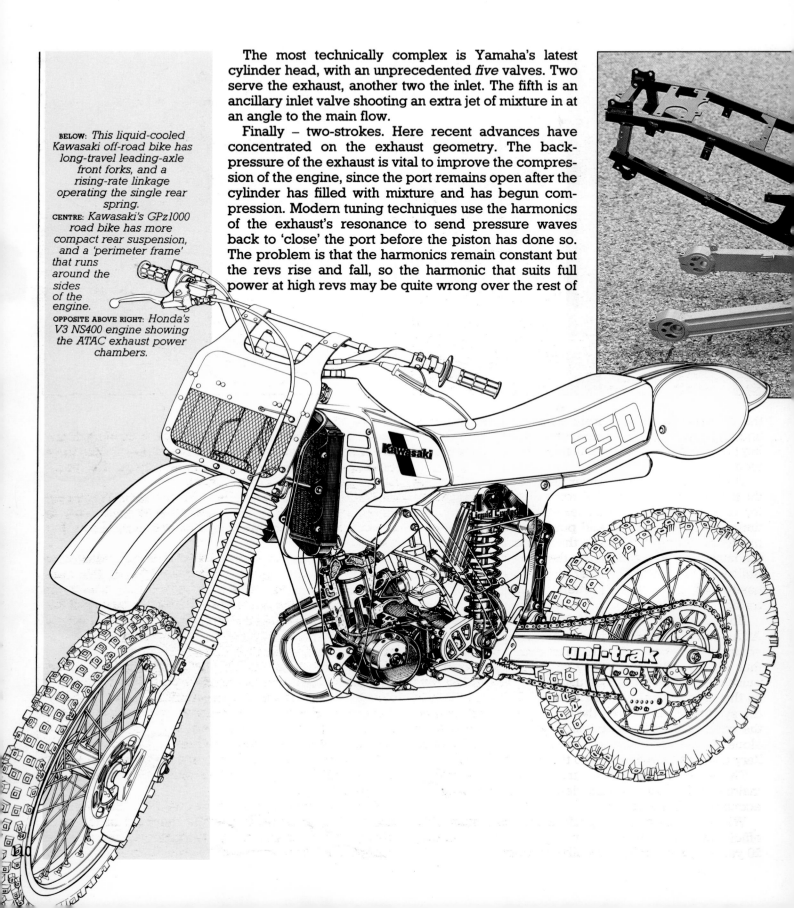

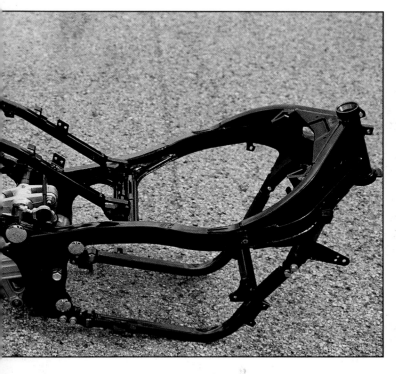

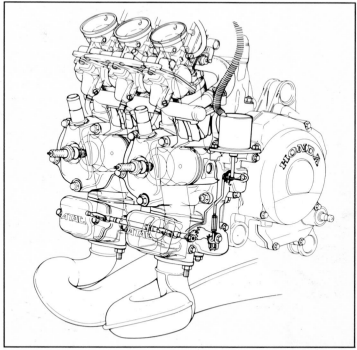

the engine's range, severely damaging performance and fuel efficiency. Designers cope with this by changing the geometry of the exhaust system in various ingenious ways.

The YPVS (Yamaha power valve system) changes the timing of the port itself. A rotating barrel valve at the top of the exhaust port is closed at low revs, giving mild timing and good bottom-end power. As the revs rise, it gradually opens to advance the port timing. This suits the faster gas flow and allows the two-stroke engine to deliver its full potential power at the top end, yet to start easily and behave well when trickling through the traffic.

Honda developed a different approach, dubbed ATAC, which leaves the port undisturbed but varies the volume of the resonating exhaust expansion chamber, thus changing the frequency of its harmonic pressure pulses. A valve on the exhaust pipe opens at low revs so that an ancillary exhaust chamber is plumbed in to the system. At high revs, the valve snaps shut, leaving the carefully profiled expansion chamber to do its job alone. Suzuki use a similar system with a smaller ancillary chamber that is cast into the cylinder barrel.

These techniques have transformed two-strokes, making their exhausts burn cleaner and improving fuel economy and rideability.

With every new model, performance improves while efficiency is enhanced. To an engine designer of only 20 years ago, it would seem like a miracle.

Frame tricks

Better engine performance could be a liability if the chassis is not good enough. The latest superbikes have developed fast in recent years to ensure that roadholding matches speed potential.

The first revolution has been in materials. Traditional drawn steel tubes have in many cases given way to aluminium – a simple and effective way of saving weight.

Designs have also evolved, particularly in relation to the rigid fixing of the steering head (flex in this area inevitably leads to wayward roadholding). The main development has been to escape from the legacy of the bicycle where the steering head is at the end of tubing in a single plane. Motorcycles have long used twin-cradle frames, so that it is at the apex of a triangle.

More recently, spurred by the Italian specialist builders Bimota, the frame has been extended forward of the steering head, so that it can be affixed from all sides. Another technique is to increase radically the angle included by the frame tubes, so that the frame tubes are now wider than the engine, passing on the outside of it rather than over the top. Examples of these are Yamaha's FJ1100/1200, and Kawasaki's perimeter frame for the GPz1000.

Anti-dive front forks are now common. This is a misnomer. It is possible to prevent the front of the bike diving, when braking, by mechanical means. The accepted practice is simply to slow down the speed at

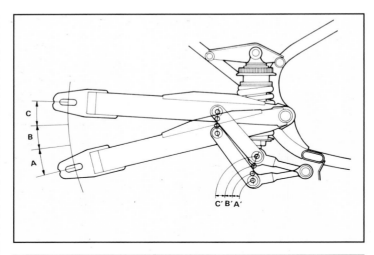

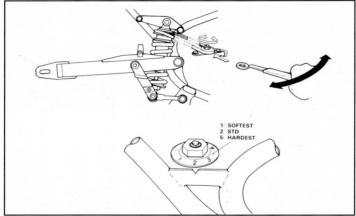

1: SOFTEST
2: STD
5: HARDEST

RIGHT: *Rising rate linkage suspension made easy. As the pivoted fork rises, the spring is compressed proportionally faster to stiffen the suspension.*
BELOW RIGHT: *Adjustment of the unit is via a remote wheel and a toothed belt.*
OPPOSITE ABOVE: *Bimota's straight tube frame extends ahead of the steering head.*
OPPOSITE CENTRE: *Complex hydraulic valving gives Kawasaki's top models progressively stiffening damping;* (OPPOSITE BELOW) *while another hydraulic sub-system is plumbed into the brakes to slow down the rate of dive when the brakes are applied.*

which it dives, by stiffening up the hydraulic damping as the brakes are applied.

This is achieved, either as in the case of Honda's torque reactive anti-dive TRAC by using a small movement of the brake caliper to operate a valve in the dampers as the brakes are applied, or by bleeding off a negligible amount of pressure in the front brake's hydraulic system to operate a similar valve.

The biggest advances have been concerned with rear suspension. Traditionally, a pivoted fork was sprung by a pair of spring/damper units, one on each side. It was Yamaha who first replaced this with a single unit, operated by a cantilevered triangulated structure, which was their monoshock derived from a much earlier system developed in Britain by Vincent-HRD.

The recent revolution has been to interpose a geometrically sophisticated system of links between the trailing pivoted fork and the spring. By careful arrangement of the bell-cranks and levers, a rising rate can easily be achieved.

This means that the middle portion of the wheel movement compresses the spring relatively less than it

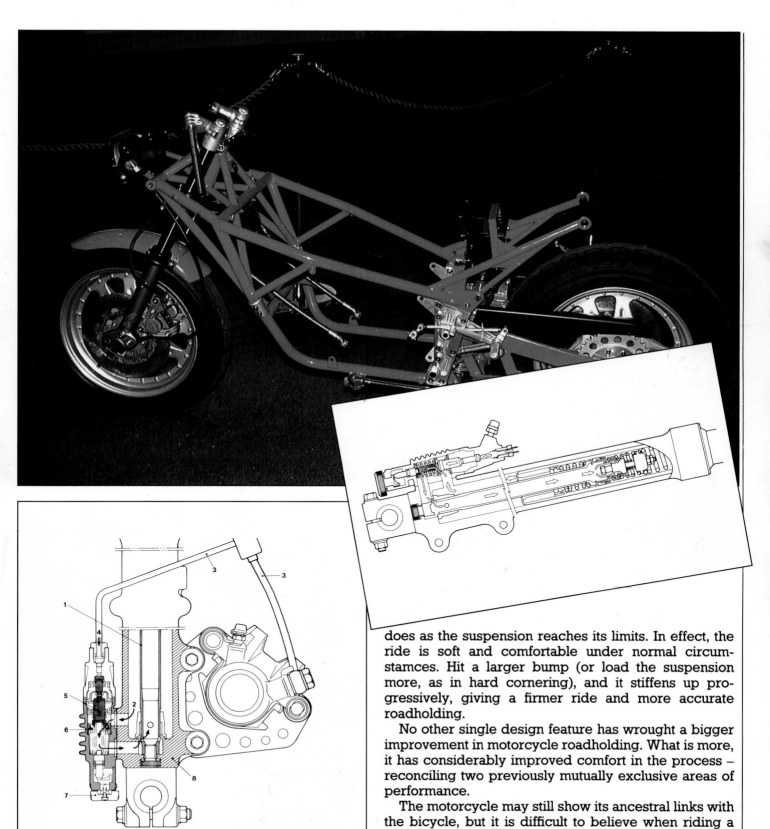

does as the suspension reaches its limits. In effect, the ride is soft and comfortable under normal circumstamces. Hit a larger bump (or load the suspension more, as in hard cornering), and it stiffens up progressively, giving a firmer ride and more accurate roadholding.

No other single design feature has wrought a bigger improvement in motorcycle roadholding. What is more, it has considerably improved comfort in the process – reconciling two previously mutually exclusive areas of performance.

The motorcycle may still show its ancestral links with the bicycle, but it is difficult to believe when riding a modern superbike.

BIKES OF THE FUTURE

F U T U R E

49ª Esposizione Internazionale Ciclo Motociclo e Accessori

PORTA EDILIZIA

T shows an unrealistic lack of respect for the motorcycles of the present to suggest that those of the near future will be significantly different.

True, the current designs still show strong links with their bicycle ancestors, both in the use of tubular frames and in their steering geometry with a high steering axis and a long front fork. It is possible to criticise them as fundamentally ill-suited to the present-day tasks of carrying heavy engines that produce more than 100 horsepower. At the same time, there is no denying that these anachronistic over-powered sprung bicycles do a remarkably efficient job, and that the superbikes of the 1980s have improved rapidly and considerably compared with those of the previous decade.

The same rate of progress would see the motor-cyclist of the 1990s riding a lighter machine, with a 750cc engine (or perhaps a supercharged 500) producing the same sort of torque and horsepower as the swiftest 1000cc machines in this book.

The frame will probably be a simple spine-type structure in steel or aluminium; the rear pivoted fork of similar structure. The front and rear suspension – far from being the interlinked pneumatic radial arms of the imagination, and in spite of a number of attractive existing alternatives – will be telescopic front forks, with a rising-rate-linkage monoshock at the rear. Unless . . .

What if things had been different from the start? What if the bicycle had never been invented? What if the motorcycle had been conceived by a car designer, fed up with the excess weight and width of his four-wheeled tin box and desirous of some *real* high performance as well as the ability to use it? (Indeed, Gottlieb Daimler's first 'car' of 1885 was more of a motor-cycle, with a pair of outrigger wheels.)

The first question the designer would ask himself is how he would sit in this new contraption. Lying on his stomach? Reclining as in a hammock? Both would be possible, but probably not as attractive as something already familiar to him; to ride it like a horse. The engine naturally falls between his knees and feet, and he is straddling the mechanical beast.

Considering the speeds the designer is contemplating, and his background in cars, he will certainly insist on at least as much protection from wind and weather as in an open sports car. He might even like the idea of being strapped into a safety capsule with a roof, with pneumatic balancing legs kicking out automatically to balance the machine at rest (he might even favour a gyroscope, operating at very low speeds to hold the machine vertical . . . useful for parking as well as stopping at the lights).

However, since he seems to be a sporting, outdoor

ABOVE: *The Quasar, with one of the authors sampling its hammock seat, is the world's only motorcycle with limited headroom.*
ABOVE RIGHT: *The Phasar, from the same designer, is also a 'Feet Forward' motorcycle.*
OPPOSITE ABOVE LEFT AND RIGHT: *The Foale QL looks bulky, but is exceptionally light. With its carbon fibre bodywork removed, the sparse frame and wishbone suspension can be seen.*

type, he will probably stay with his preconceptions of the horse, and choose to sit outside of the main bodywork (though behind a comprehensive and aerodynamic fairing) and to wear protective clothes to beat the weather. As with the horse it is better, if you fall off, to be well clear of the beast, so there would be no question of safety belts.

Having organized the distribution of motorcycle and rider, and allowed for a modicum of secure luggage stowage space, the designer will turn to the construction. His car background will tell him to make the bodywork and the chassis in a single complex structure, a monocoque. Pressed steel would be the chosen material, or would be if he was planning to build a large number. For this first prototype, though, or for a small production run, he will construct it of welded tubes, and the bodywork of moulded glass- and carbon-fibre. The frame will hug the engine, coming in close ahead and behind. This is in order to provide location for the suspension pivots.

It is absolutely certain that an engineer with a clean sheet of paper would not choose to design telescopic forks. Instead, he would probably look at car front suspensions and soon decide that the best alternative was a double-wishbone set-up, with the steering axis in the centre of the wheel. This could follow racing car practice but with the wheel 'upright' pivoted at each end in line with the wheel centre. It could be placed above the wheel, with both ends within a dished wheel, or even straddling these two points via an arced upright.

Common sense and design economy would dictate feeding the suspension loads in as close to the centre of the structure as possible. Instead of a long frame run-

ning alongside the front wheel, with the wishbones sideways to it, as in a car, he would turn the design through 90 degrees so that they pointed forwards, and were pivoted on the frame ahead of the engine. They would then need to be arced, to bypass the wheel on full steering lock. Thus the wheel would be unencumbered on one side, with a pair of wishbones modified into C-shaped leading arms on the other.

For the rear suspension, a single trailing arm would suffice, containing the shaft drive. A single suspension unit would be operated by a linkage, to provide a rising rate: comfortable at first, and firming up progressively as it was compressed.

The bike would be steered by a pair of levers, held like the handles of a revolver. As the feet would be needed to balance the machine, these levers would have to incorporate controls for the clutch, accelerator, brakes, and starter (just in case of stalling at a red light).

The seat would be arranged above the frame, and the bodywork would allow free access to it, while shielding the rider from the high-speed blast of air and weather. Naturally, it would be designed for the optimum aerodynamic penetration, as well as to aid stability at high speed by providing some downforce.

With all this the designer would be ready to show the rest of the world in their cars a thing or two about acceleration and agility. The finished machine would look a cross between a bullet and a modern superbike, in spite of being fundamentally different in its evolutionary starting point. While the Japanese churn out bicycle-replicas by the hundreds of thousands, a handful of creative engineers are exploring ideas very similar to these. It is anything but far fetched.

True to its reputation for amiable eccentricity, Great Britain is a natural home to these people. It was in Britain in the 1970s that the first motorcycle with a roof was sold to the public. The Quasar offered a number of radically new alternatives all in one – the roof, so to speak, capping them all. The Quasar was the most successful of a breed of motorcycle called 'Feet Forward', in which the rider reclines in something resembling a hammock. With a body shaped like an arrow, it used a tubular frame with Earle's fork front suspension. Though it cruised economically and rapidly, its drawback was a pedestrian 750cc Reliant car engine that left it breathless compared with the power of a real superbike.

Later, the same designer, Malcolm Newell, remedied this. His Phasar used a twin-cam Kawasaki Z1300 engine, and had an open cockpit, like a World War One fighter. With its small frontal area and streamlined bodywork it could reach 130mph with astonishing speed.

In the meantime, others were exploring wishbone suspension. A racer called Norman Hossack, late of Maclaren car Formula One racing team, put the wishbones above the wheel, with what looked like old-fashioned 'girder' forks in fact performing the role of an extended wheel upright.

In another small workshop, long-time front-fork iconoclast Tony Foale was developing a different wishbone-type arrangement, which was radical also in that it disposed by example of a number of the sacred cows of motorcycle geometry. The lower wishbone on his QL (Quantum Leap) was C-shaped, and curved in to the centre of the wheel. The upright rose to above the

ABOVE AND ABOVE RIGHT: *Bimota's 'Tesi' uses all-new design with leading-arm front suspension that looks simple but is surprisingly complex.*
OPPOSITE RIGHT: *Hossack design offers wishbone suspension to fit onto a conventional bike frame.*

FOLLOWING PAGE: *Shaped like a cigar, with miles of sand ahead — Alex MacFadzean sets out on a trial on his Suzuki powered Penetrator. The Pendine Sands in Wales are an historic site for record attempts.*

centre of the tyre, where the top wishbone provided location.

Simultaneously, in France, ex-Renault Formula One designers were working along similar lines to build a radical grand prix racing machine. Known as the Elf, after its sponsors, this made arcs out of both wishbones, with the upright within the deeply dished wheel. An endurance racing version had appeared promising but unreliable at a few Le Mans 24-hour races, and when the Grand Prix version appeared in 1985 it plainly required more development before it could challenge the existing order of telescopic-forked machines from Honda, Yamaha and Suzuki.

There is enough appeal in the idea to attract others in Europe as well. The Italian firm Bimota, already famous for improving on the existing type of frame structure, are among those researching new designs. They are developing the Tesi (Theory), using a single leading arm up front to provide hub-centre steering, with the steering transmitted hydraulically.

The biggest possible sign that the days of the telescopic fork may be numbered came at the 1985 Tokyo Motor Show. There, Suzuki showed the Falcorustyco, stunning not so much for its hub-centre steering and revolutionary styling (which had already been seen in Europe), but for the fact that it was shown by one of the major Japanese manufacturers. Until now, although innovative in detail and in engine design, they have remained conservative in matters of fundamental approach, and since, by force of sales strength, it is the Japanese who dictate the direction of the market, this may be a very significant motorcycle indeed.

THE RECORD BREAKERS

ABOVE: *The American Freddie Spencer riding a Honda on his way to winning the 1985 500cc World Championship.*

ABOVE: *The 1985 250cc World Champion Freddie Spencer on his Honda.*

PAST 500CC WORLD CHAMPIONS

Year	Rider	Manufacturer
1949	Leslie Graham (British, AJS)	AJS
1950	Umberto Masetti (Italian, Gilera)	Gilera
1951	Geoff Duke (British, Norton)	Norton
1952	Umberto Masetti (Italian, Gilera)	Gilera
1953	Geoff Duke (British, Gilera)	Gilera
1954	Geoff Duke (British, Gilera)	Gilera
1955	Geoff Duke (British, Gilera)	Gilera
1956	John Surtees (British, MV Augusta)	MV Augusta
1957	Libero Liberati (Italian, Gilera)	Gilera
1958	John Surtees (British, MV Augusta)	MV Augusta
1959	John Surtees (British, MV Augusta)	MV Augusta
1960	John Surtees (British, MV Augusta)	MV Augusta
1961	Gary Hocking (Rhodesian, MV Augusta)	MV Augusta
1962	Mike Hailwood (British, MV Augusta)	MV Augusta
1963	Mike Hailwood (British, MV Augusta)	MV Augusta
1964	Mike Hailwood (British, MV Augusta)	MV Augusta
1965	Mike Hailwood (British, MV Augusta)	MV Augusta
1966	Giacomo Agostini (Italian, MV Augusta)	MV Augusta
1967	Giacomo Agostini (Italian, MV Augusta)	MV Augusta
1968	Giacomo Agostini (Italian, MV Augusta)	MV Augusta
1969	Giacomo Agostini (Italian, MV Augusta)	MV Augusta
1970	Giacomo Agostini (Italian, MV Augusta)	MV Augusta
1971	Giacomo Agostini (Italian, MV Augusta)	MV Augusta
1972	Giacomo Agostini (Italian, MV Augusta)	MV Augusta
1973	Phil Read (British, MV Augusta)	MV Augusta
1974	Phil Read (British, MV Augusta)	MV Augusta
1975	Giacomo Agostini (Italian, Yamaha)	Yamaha
1976	Barry Sheene (British, Suzuki)	Suzuki
1977	Barry Sheene (British, Suzuki)	Suzuki
1978	Kenny Roberts (American, Yamaha)	Yamaha
1979	Kenny Roberts (American, Yamaha)	Yamaha
1980	Kenny Roberts (American, Yamaha)	Yamaha
1981	Marco Lucchinelli (Italian, Suzuki)	Suzuki
1982	Franco Uncini (Italian, Suzuki)	Suzuki
1983	Freddie Spencer (American, Honda)	Honda
1984	Eddie Lawson (American, Yamaha)	Yamaha
1985	Freddie Spencer (American, Honda)	Honda

PAST 250CC WORLD CHAMPIONS

Year	Rider	Manufacturer
1949	Bruno Ruffo (Italian, Moto Guzzi)	Moto Guzzi
1950	Dario Ambrosini (Italian, Benelli)	Benelli
1951	Bruno Ruffo (Italian, Moto Guzzi)	Moto Guzzi
1952	Enrico Lorenzetti (Italian, Moto Guzzi)	Moto Guzzi
1953	Werner Haas (West German, NSU)	NSU
1954	Werner Haas (West German, NSU)	NSU
1955	Hermann Müller (West German, NSU)	NSU
1956	Carlo Ubbiali (Italian, MV Augusta)	MV Augusta
1957	Cecil Sandford (British, Mondial)	Mondial
1958	Tarquinio Provini (Italian, MV Augusta)	MV Augusta
1959	Carlo Ubbiali (Italian, MV Augusta)	MV Augusta
1960	Carlo Ubbiali (Italian, MV Augusta)	MV Augusta
1961	Mike Hailwood (British, Honda)	Honda
1962	Jim Redman (Rhodesian, Honda)	Honda
1963	Jim Redman (Rhodesian, Honda)	Honda
1964	Phil Read (British, Yamaha)	Yamaha
1965	Phil Read (British, Yamaha)	Yamaha
1966	Mike Hailwood (British, Honda)	Honda
1967	Mike Hailwood (British, Honda)	Honda
1968	Phil Read (British, Yamaha)	Yamaha
1969	Kel Carruthers (Australian, Benelli)	Benelli
1970	Rod Gould (British, Yamaha)	Yamaha
1971	Phil Read (British, Yamaha)	Yamaha
1972	Jarno Saarinen (Finnish, Yamaha)	Yamaha
1973	Dieter Braun (West German, Yamaha)	Yamaha
1974	Walter Villa (Italian, Harley-Davidson)	Harley-Davidson
1975	Walter Villa (Italian, Harley-Davidson)	Harley-Davidson
1976	Walter Villa (Italian, Harley-Davidson)	Harley-Davidson
1977	Mario Lega (Italian, Morbidelli)	Morbidelli
1978	Kork Ballington (South African, Kawasaki)	Kawasaki
1979	Kork Ballington (South African, Kawasaki)	Kawasaki
1980	Anton Mang (West German, Kawasaki)	Kawasaki
1981	Anton Mang (West German, Kawasaki)	Kawasaki
1982	Jean-Louis Tournadre (French, Yamaha)	Yamaha
1983	Carlos Lavado (Yugoslavian, Yamaha)	Yamaha
1984	Christian Sarron (French, Yamaha)	Yamaha
1985	Freddie Spencer (American, Honda)	Honda

ABOVE: *Fausto Gresini riding a Garelli, winner of the 1985 125cc World Championship.*

ABOVE: *The Dutch pair Streuer and Schnieders riding a Yamaha on their way to becoming the 1985 World Sidecar Champions.*

PAST 125CC WORLD CHAMPIONS

Year	Rider	Manufacturer
1949	Nello Pagani (Italian, Mondial)	Mondial
1950	Bruno Ruffo (Italian, Mondial)	Mondial
1951	Carlo Ubbiali (Italian, Mondial)	Mondial
1952	Cecil Sandford (British, MV Augusta)	MV Augusta
1953	Werner Haas (West German, NSU)	NSU
1954	Rupert Hollaus (Austrian, NSU)	NSU
1955	Carlo Ubbiali (Italian, MV Augusta)	MV Augusta
1956	Carlo Ubbiali (Italian, MV Augusta)	MV Augusta
1957	Tarquinio Provini (Italian, Mondial)	Mondial
1958	Carlo Ubbiali (Italian, MV Augusta)	MV Augusta
1959	Carlo Ubbiali (Italian, MV Augusta)	MV Augusta
1960	Carlo Ubbiali (Italian, MV Augusta)	MV Augusta
1961	Tom Phillis (Australian, Honda)	Honda
1962	Luigi Taveri (Swiss, Honda)	Honda
1963	Hugh Anderson (New Zealander, Suzuki)	Suzuki
1964	Luigi Taveri (Swiss, Honda)	Honda
1965	Hugh Anderson (New Zealander, Suzuki)	Suzuki
1966	Luigi Taveri (Swiss, Honda)	Honda
1967	Bill Ivy (British, Yamaha)	Yamaha
1968	Phil Read (British, Yamaha)	Yamaha
1969	Dave Simmonds (British, Kawasaki)	Kawasaki
1970	Dieter Braun (West German, Suzuki)	Suzuki
1971	Angel Nieto (Spanish, Derbi)	Derbi
1972	Angel Nieto (Spanish, Derbi)	Derbi
1973	Kent Andersson (Swedish, Yamaha)	Yamaha
1974	Kent Andersson (Swedish, Yamaha)	Yamaha
1975	Paolo Pileri (Italian, Morbidelli)	Morbidelli
1976	Pier Paolo Bianchi (Italian, Morbidelli)	Morbidelli
1977	Pier Paolo Bianchi (Italian, Morbidelli)	Morbidelli
1978	Eugenio Lazzarini (Italian, MBA)	MBA
1979	Angel Nieto (Spanish, Minarelli)	Minarelli
1980	Pier Paolo Bianchi (Italian, MBA)	MBA
1981	Angel Nieto (Spanish, Minarelli)	Minarelli
1982	Angel Nieto (Spanish, Garelli)	Garelli
1983	Angel Nieto (Spanish, Garelli)	Garelli
1984	Angel Nieto (Spanish, Garelli)	Garelli
1985	Fausto Gresini (Italian, Garelli)	Garelli

PAST SIDECAR WORLD CHAMPIONS

Year	Rider	Manufacturer
1949	E. Oliver, D. Jenkinson (British)	Norton
1950	E. Oliver (British), L. Dobelli (Italian)	Norton
1951	E. Oliver (British), L. Dobelli (Italian)	Norton
1952	C. Smith, B. Clements (British)	Norton
1953	E. Oliver, S. Dibben (British)	Norton
1954	W. Noll, F. Cron (West German)	BMW
1955	W. Faust, K. Remmert (West German)	BMW
1956	W. Noll, F. Cron (West German)	BMW
1957	F. Hillebrand, M. Grunwald (West German)	BMW
1958	W. Schneider, H. Strauss (West German)	BMW
1959	W. Schneider, H. Strauss (West German)	BMW
1960	H. Fath, A. Wohligemuth (West German)	BMW
1961	M. Deubel, E. Horner (West German)	BMW
1962	M. Deubel, E. Horner (West German)	BMW
1963	M. Deubel, E. Horner (West German)	BMW
1964	M. Deubel, E. Horner (West German)	BMW
1965	F. Scheidegger (Swiss), J. Robinson (British)	BMW
1966	F. Scheidegger (Swiss), J. Robinson (British)	BMW
1967	K. Enders, R. Engelhardt (West German)	BMW
1968	H. Fath, W. Kallaugh (West German)	URS
1969	K. Enders, R. Engelhardt (West German)	BMW
1970	K. Enders, W. Kallaugh (West German)	BMW
1971	H. Owesle (German), P. Rutterford (British)	URS Fath
1972	K. Enders, R. Engelhardt (West German)	BMW
1973	K. Enders, R. Engelhardt (West German)	BMW
1974	K. Enders, R. Engelhardt (West German)	Bosch BMW
1975	R. Steinhausen, J. Huber (West German)	Bosch Konig
1976	R. Steinhausen, J. Huber (West German)	Bosch Konig
1977	G. O'Dell, K. Arthur, C. Holland (British)	Yamaha
1978	R. Biland (Swiss), K. Williams (British)	Yamaha
1979	B2A R. Biland, K. Waltisperg (Swiss)	Yamaha
1979	B2B B. Holzer, K. Meierhans (Swiss)	Yamaha
1980	J. Taylor (British), B. Johansson (Swedish)	Yamaha
1981	R. Biland, K. Waltisperg (Swiss)	Yamaha
1982	W. Schwarzel, A. Huber (West German)	Yamaha
1983	R. Biland, K. Waltisperg (Swiss)	Yamaha
1984	E. Streuer, B. Schnieders (Dutch)	Yamaha
1985	E. Streuer, B. Schnieders (Dutch)	Yamaha

INDEX

Page numbers in *italic* refer to illustrations and captions

127